STRESS AND YOUR STOMACH

DR VERNON COLEMAN worked as a GP in the Midlands for ten years, and is now a professional author and broadcaster. He was the UK's first TV 'agony uncle', and has written over thirty books explaining medicine to the lay reader, including *How to Stop Feeling Guilty*, *Women's Problems – an A–Z*, *Overcoming Stress* and *Bodypower* for Sheldon Press. Dr Coleman is a Fellow of the Royal Society of Medicine and lives in a cottage on the North Devon coast. His magazine and newspaper columns are read regularly by millions of readers around the world, and his books have been translated into eleven languages and have sold well over a million copies.

Overcoming Common Problems

A successful and popular series to give you practical
help for the emotional and medical problems of
everyday life.

Paperbacks £1·95 to £4·95
Available from all good bookshops

For a complete list of titles write to;
Sheldon Press Mail Order,
SPCK, Marylebone Road, London NW1 4DU

Overcoming Common Problems

STRESS AND YOUR STOMACH

Dr Vernon Coleman

SHELDON PRESS
LONDON

First published in Great Britain in 1983 by
Sheldon Press, SPCK, Marylebone Road, London NW1 4DU

Second impression 1989

British Library Cataloguing in Publication Data

Coleman, Vernon
Stress and your stomach — (Overcoming common
problems)
1. Stomach   2. Stress (Psychology)
I. Title   II. Series
612 32   RC816

ISBN 0-85969-375-9

Typeset by Memo Typography Ltd
Nicosia, Cyprus
Printed in Great Britian by
Richard Clay (The Chaucer Press) Ltd,
Bungay, Suffolk

Contents

Note

This book is not intended as a substitute for the medical advice of physicians. The reader should consult a physician in all matters relating to health and particularly in respect of any symptoms that may require diagnosis or medical attention. While the advice and information here are believed to be true neither the author nor the publisher can accept any legal responsibility or liability for any errors or omissions that may be made.

VERNON COLEMAN
is an author
and general medical practitioner

Introduction

Gastrointestinal problems are common worldwide and they are becoming commoner. There are in all millions of people in the developed countries of the world who regularly suffer from stomach complaints such as indigestion, gastritis and peptic ulceration. It is said that if five people sit down to dinner one of them will suffer from indigestion afterwards.

To help sufferers cope there are countless products on the market. The sales of over-the-counter remedies for stomach upsets rise annually and each year the major drug companies introduce many new products designed to help doctors deal with such problems as indigestion, gastritis and peptic ulceration.

Unfortunately, most of the remedies which exist and which are sold by drug companies or advocated by doctors are designed basically to relieve the symptoms and deal with the damage that has already been done. And while these solutions will often provide temporary relief it is, I'm afraid, quite true to say that in many cases the relief will be just that — temporary. Within months or even weeks the symptoms will have recurred and the sufferer will be no better off.

I believe that there is convincing evidence that the majority of stomach symptoms are either caused or exacerbated by stress and that consequently a long-term solution to the problem can be obtained by concentrating on the cause rather than the effect. In this book I intend to show why I believe that so many stomach symptoms are associated with stress, what sort of problems cause stress and precisely how stress can be controlled and those symptoms can best be relieved.

1

The Nature of Stress

Although the subject of stress has been discussed in a great many different magazines and newspapers over the years there are still many misconceptions about precisely what stress is and what sort of people suffer from it.

Even the very word 'stress' is the subject of much confusion, for some people use it to describe the sort of activity, pressure and strain that cause mental anguish and physical damage, while others use it as a general term to describe the physiological response to pressure. In this book I have used the word stress to refer to the sort of pressures that cause problems rather than the physical and mental problems themselves. I have used the phrase 'stress-induced disease' to refer to disorders produced by stress.

Who suffers from stress?

If you asked the average man or woman in the street to describe the sort of individual he thought might be most likely to suffer from too much stress he would probably mention taxi-drivers, airline pilots, air traffic controllers and business executives. Indeed I suspect that some people imagine that stress is something endured almost exclusively by harassed businessmen rushing from airport to airport, clutching alligator cases stuffed to the twin brass combination locks with documents and contracts.

In practice, of course, it is quite impossible to classify stress sufferers by occupation or by any other criterion. The simple truth is that anyone can suffer from too much stress and it is the individual's *susceptibility* to stress rather than the *extent* of the stress which governs the amount of damage that is done.

Some people are extremely vulnerable to stress and they will suffer a good deal from a fairly minimal amount of pressure. Other individuals, in contrast, are capable of withstanding enormous pressures without suffering any ill-effects at all and may indeed seem to thrive as the pressure builds up. This is not, of course, a phenomenon which is peculiar to stress. It is just as true to say that some people are more susceptible than others to colds.

Nevertheless, despite the fact that there is a good deal of individual variation in susceptibility to stress it is a fact that there are some situations and some pressures which are particularly likely to produce stress-induced disease. These situations and pressures are rarely connected to individual occupations but are more general, and can as easily affect a nurse or a shop assistant as a company director or high-level business executive.

What causes stress? Variations on a theme

It isn't possible to list all the different stresses and strains which can cause damage. But on the following pages of this short, introductory section I have tried to describe some of the types of stress most likely to produce problems. In particular, I have tried to suggest some of the less obvious ways in which we can all find ourselves under pressure.

These sources of distress are included in this book simply as an introduction to the subject. Most readers could undoubtedly add many more sources of stress to the list and there is a more comprehensive checklist on page 54.

Ways to deal with these pressures and the pains they produce are discussed in the final three chapters of the book.

The pressure to achieve

The pressure to achieve starts very early these days. The youngest patient I've ever seen with indigestion was just eight years old and he had acquired his gastrointestinal symptoms simply because his parents and schoolteachers had put him under too much pressure.

From the age of six, Robert was expected to do at least an

hour's homework every evening and at the weekends he was shut into his bedroom for at least two hours every Saturday and Sunday. The pressure on young Robert to do well in all his academic subjects was matched only by the pressure on him to do well at sports. When he wasn't studying Robert was kept busy with extra coaching in cricket, football and athletics. The aim was clearly not to take part but to win. Robert was encouraged to keep a poster recording his athletic achievements in his bedroom.

All this was just too much, and when he was eight years old Robert began to complain of regular symptoms of indigestion. Investigations showed that there was no sign of any peptic ulceration, but there was little doubt in the mind of the specialist who examined Robert that if things went on as they were a peptic ulcer would be the next logical development.

Although Robert's problems were perhaps slightly more serious than those of any other children I've seen with stress problems his history is by no means unique. It is in fact extremely common these days for young children to be put under an unbearable amount of pressure to do well at school. The pressure is applied by both parents and schoolteachers and it covers sports and games as well as academic subjects.

It sometimes seems to me that hardly anyone plays games for fun any more, and there are today so many junior leagues and junior cups that even five- and six-year-olds are encouraged to take their sports very seriously.

The same, of course, is quite true of adults who also seem to take their sports and games very seriously these days. A few years ago most of the men and women who played games no more than once or twice a week would really enjoy themselves, would describe themselves as merely social players and would relax on the squash court, the golf course or the football pitch. They would enjoy the camaraderie and the chance to do something different for a change as much as they would enjoy the competition. Today I find myself amazed whenever I go anywhere near a sports club of any kind. The people playing golf are worrying desperately about their handicaps, their positions in the club team and their latest scores. The squash players are to be found poring over instruction manuals and video recordings of their own games; and the football players are plunged into despair if they fail to pick up a trophy every season.

This desire to do well at everything, and to be *seen* to be doing well, is endemic in our modern society. The young executive who isn't ambitious is considered rather odd, and the man who enjoys his job knows that he will be uncomfortable if he rises any higher in his company hierarchy, and refuses an unwanted promotion, will be considered irrational and very probably mentally ill rather than sensible and very sane.

The pressure to achieve begins to affect many of us at an early age; and it continues to affect us throughout our lives.

Religion: a question of belief

It may seem strange to suggest that religion can be a cause of stress—after all one of the traditional purposes of religion is to calm and soothe, to support and to provide guidance. But whatever the ideals and theoretical purposes of religion may be the simple truth is, I'm afraid, that religion is a common and very significant cause of stress in a great many people.

I could justify that claim in a number of different ways but the simplest and perhaps the most obvious way is to describe one particular patient of mine who suffered greatly because of her religious beliefs.

Although she looked considerably older Mrs Harkness was in her late twenties when I first met her. She had two small children and a husband to look after and all three seemed to lean on her a great deal. Before her marriage she had worked as a secretary in a building firm and she had a tremendous figure and a personality to match. She'd given up work when she was expecting her first child and although she had intended to go back to work later on she seemed to have few hopes of ever doing that when she joined my list of patients.

She'd given up her ambition to return to work because her

4

second child had been born mentally handicapped and much of her life was spent in providing simple nursing care. She knew very well that her son, an unlucky victim of the whooping cough vaccine, was unlikely ever to manage to fend for himself.

All that may sound quite enough of a burden for one woman but Mrs Harkness had another huge problem to try and deal with. She was a Roman Catholic and her problem was that although she couldn't bear the idea of having any more children her Church taught that she would be quite wrong to use any form of contraception.

To begin with she trusted to luck and simply prayed every night not to get pregnant again. For a while it worked quite well, but one month she had a scare, was two weeks late with her period, and all her early terror of a third pregnancy returned.

That was more than enough for her. After that she refused to allow her husband to touch her and for three months she slept in the same bed as her mentally handicapped child. Each week when she saw the priest she asked him to allow her to use some form of contraception and each week he simply repeated what she already knew; that to use contraceptives would be to go against God and to incur the wrath of the Church.

Eventually the predictable happened and her husband had an affair with a divorced woman who worked as a barmaid in a local men's club. It wasn't so much a serious love affair as a simple case of bipartisan lust, but it upset Mrs Harkness enough to convince her that she really ought to allow her husband back into her bed.

Whether the intervening period had made her more fertile or her God had acquired a more than mischievous sense of humour that single episode led to Mrs Harkness's third pregnancy.

To begin with Mrs Harkness was hysterical. She insisted that she couldn't possibly cope with a third child, that she couldn't go through with another pregnancy. She sobbed and cried and pleaded for help.

Eventually, after she'd been interviewed several times by both an obstetrician and a psychiatrist she was offered an abortion. She accepted the offer immediately, had an abortion and returned home to the rage and disapproval of both her husband and her priest. They told her that she had sinned against God, that she was guilty of murder and that she would be damned for eternity.

Three weeks after the abortion she was admitted to hospital with a bleeding peptic ulcer, and four days later she died. The surgeon who had looked after her insisted that she had willed herself to death. He firmly believed that if she had had the slightest desire to live she would have survived.

I believe that Mrs Harkness could have survived if her only task had been to look after her family. She could even have managed to look after her mentally handicapped child without too much difficulty. But the pressure of trying to reconcile her own needs, the needs of her husband and the teachings of the Church proved too much for her. For Mrs Harkness her faith was a burden she couldn't carry; it was directly responsible for a dilemma she couldn't solve, and by producing the pressure and stress which led to the development of her peptic ulcer, and the concomitant absence of any will to live, it led directly to her death.

Personal relationships

When any close relationship between two people comes to an end the result can be catastrophic. The end of a love affair, the end of a marriage or the end of a friendship can all be extremely damaging in terms of the amount of stress they can produce. Obviously the closer the relationship the greater the damage that is done when the relationship comes to an end.

But it is not only when relationships end that stress is produced. In a marriage where the two partners are no longer in love with one another, or perhaps even more important when they no longer even *like* one another, the stresses and strains can be severe enough to produce any number of mental and physical problems.

Take Alan Kent, for example, who came to see me with clear

6

and unmistakable signs of an early stomach ulcer, and told me how he and his wife had lived in a state of permanent feud for the better part of a year.

There hadn't been any particular reason for their falling out of love and into anger. In Mr Kent's own words 'it just seemed to happen over the years'. But whatever the cause may have been the effect was pretty daunting. Slowly over the months each partner had taken to nibbling at the other in the most hurtful and damaging way. Since they had not so long before been madly in love with one another they both knew where to bite in order to cause the maximum amount of pain.

Personal relationships are vital to us all. It is from our relationships with others that most of us obtain our strength. But personal relationships that have gone sour for any reason can be a source of unending distress. And on the whole the closer the relationship is to start with the more acute the distress can be if it fails.

Pressure at work

When we think of individuals who suffer from pressure at work we usually think of executives, company directors and others with too much responsibility. However, while it is of course true that people in positions of great power often do suffer from stress it is also true that those who work for them can often find themselves suffering from stress-induced diseases.

The individual who is being pushed and harried by an ambitious executive may suffer as may an individual making his way up the ladder and struggling to satisfy his superiors all the time. As always it is not so much the type of stress or the nature of the work involved that is important as the attitude of the individual concerned and his capacity to cope with whatever levels of stress he may be expected to endure.

The Micawber principle

There are relatively few people in our society who are in genuine danger of starving to death because they cannot afford to buy enough food to eat, or of freezing to death because they don't have any shelter or enough money to pay for basic heating.

But there are a great many people who are quite genuinely worried and distressed because they cannot cope with money problems. Some of those individuals suffer because for one reason or another their income is totally inadequate to enable them to cope with ordinary living expenses. Some individuals suffer because they are unable to handle money with care or proper thought. And some suffer because through no real fault of their own they are hit by unexpected demands and expenses.

More numerous than individuals in these categories, however, and perhaps even more likely to suffer from stress-induced illnesses as a result of their financial problems, are those people who have an adequate income but who for one reason or another struggle to live beyond their means.

Encouraged to spend and to buy items that they may not need or even want, many people who could theoretically live comfortably on their earnings, push themselves into debt. Seduced by the major banks who regularly buy advertising encouraging people to borrow money to pay for luxury items, these individuals push themselves further and further into debt and deeper into trouble. Encouraged by easy-term hire purchase arrangements they buy equipment they don't need with money they haven't got.

If one partner in a marriage wants to spend and the other wants to save then the agonies and pressures can mount even more rapidly. The partner who wants to spend will accuse the partner who wants to save of being mean and miserly while the one who wants to save will accuse the other of being profligate and careless. Whatever the end result may be the consequences in terms of the partnership can be devastating.

Sexual problems

Few causes of stress are as invasive or as ubiquitous as sex. It gets everywhere, affects everything, and has an overall influence far greater than any of us might imagine were we to try and assess its status and significance in our lives.

Sex is, for example, one of the main weapons used by advertising copywriters, packagers and marketing men. It is more difficult to think of an item that isn't sold with the aid of sex than to think of one that is.

Even when the advertising doesn't obviously and directly use sex to sell us a product, sex is usually in there somewhere. Advertisements for soap and mouthwashes, for example, will usually imply that if you don't use the right product you'll be unlikely to attract the partner of your choice.

All this advertising pressure produces results, of course. But it doesn't just sell the products that it is designed to sell. It also encourages a wide range of suspicions, fears and fantasies about sex.

It is, for example, not at all unknown for individuals to consider themselves to be in some way exceptional or odd because they do not spend their days thinking about sex and their nights practising what they have been thinking. And with the pressure from the advertisers allied with the pressure from all those sex marketeers who have a commercial interest in selling us sexual delights of every possible kind it is hardly surprising that there are today a great many men and women who worry because their own sexual activities are seemingly unexceptional both in quality and quantity.

Indeed, it is, in my experience, far more common for individuals to be worried about the fact that they don't seem to be as interested in sex or as determined to experiment in sexual matters as they think they ought to be than it is for people to be worried by a genuine equipment failure of some kind. The majority of people think they have a sexual problem only because their own attitudes, sexual ambitions and yearnings don't match up to the attitudes, ambitions and yearnings that they think they ought to experience. The advertisers and the marketeers have between them created a new type of pressure and produced a whole new range of sexual problems.

Problems specific to women: The other sexual problem which can't be ignored is nothing to do with raw sexuality but is instead a product of the fairly modern liberation movement.

During recent years a growing number of women have begun to demand and expect to be treated as individuals with rights and responsibilities of their own rather than to be treated simply as companions, wives or mistresses. Quite justifiably those women who have taken an active part in the emancipation movement have campaigned for equality in all areas of living.

Unfortunately, the problems which have arisen from this type of campaign have affected both women and men and have produced many heartaches and much concern.

Women who might a few years ago have been relatively content simply to regard themselves as mothers and housewives now feel that if they are to live their lives to the full they should be entitled to enjoy a career outside the home. This has nothing to do with the need for extra money (although that is obviously another possible cause of stress) but is simply a question of achieving status as an individual human being.

The problem is, of course, that many of the women who have recently tried to combine looking after a home with resuming a career have found themselves torn between their two sets of duties. On the one hand they have been anxious to carve out for themselves some sort of personal career. On the other hand they have found themselves struggling to satisfy the demands of their husbands and families. The amount of guilt and the amount of stress produced by that guilt has been enormous.

At the same time a large number of men have found themselves facing almost identical problems. They have been conscious of the fact that they have a duty to allow their wives to run their own lives and yet they have still felt a duty to provide and to be protective. All that, mixed with the fact that they have had to do their own washing, cooking and ironing has produced some very considerable psychological problems.

The environment

Our ancestors had to live in surroundings far less well organized than our own and it does seem somehow to be rather churlish if we complain about the stressful nature of the environment in which we live. It looks as though we are just being difficult to please if we complain that life in a big, modern city with its piped electricity, water and music is as stressful as life was in, say, a small medieval town with primitive sewage facilities, unmade roads and no public facilities to speak of.

And yet I do believe that life in a modern, big city is probably more stressful than life in those relatively primitive surroundings. There are several reasons for this, of course. Our own demands and expectations, and those of the people around us are very different to the demands of our ancestors. The pace of modern living is much faster. And the number of problems and pressures is considerably greater today than it was a few centuries ago.

Stress in a modern city: But the biggest cause of stress in a modern city is the fact that so many of the things which cause pressure are out of our own control. If you live in a town where the roads are badly made, and you know that they are badly made, then you get accustomed to getting your feet muddy and you either get used to that or you wear something to protect your feet. Paved roads don't exist so there is no solution to the problem as far as you are concerned. You must do the best that you can to make life bearable and to minimize the amount of stress. Similarly if there isn't any public sewage system then you must make your own arrangements. You dig your own hole and when it is full you dig another. The problem is soluble and you are not reliant on anyone else. When you need heat you chop up wood, and when you run out of wood you chop up more. You know precisely what you have to do to maintain your living standard and your reliance on others is very limited.

In a modern city, however, things are very different. The problems and the pressures are neither easily solved nor are they

11

easily dismissed. Many continue to irritate and annoy from day to day. Our reliance on one another, for example, means that when something goes wrong with the plumbing, or when there is an electricity strike, or when the garbage is not collected, problems sprout alarmingly. The absence of electricity can mean an absence of heat and light, and since we have all grown to be dependent upon piped facilities such as electricity our capacity to cope when that supply is withdrawn is severely limited. With things out of our control the problems produce stresses of almost incalculable magnitude.

In the days when people who wanted to travel from one place to another had either to walk or ride on horseback, there were enormous problems in travelling long distances. But those problems were easily defined and everyone knew what they were. Expectations were very limited, and it was up to the individual himself to make his own arrangements to travel.

Today most of us travel more in a week than our ancestors would have travelled in a year. We expect to be able to travel fairly long distances in fairly short periods of time. We become very stressed if for any reason there is a breakdown in the transport system or a traffic queue causes a hold-up. Our personal expectations are high but our capacity to do anything to ensure that our expectations are met is strictly limited. If the trains aren't running, or the buses aren't available, or there is a strike at the airport, then there are no simple solutions to the many problems which result. If you're stuck in a traffic jam twenty miles away from the office then there is nothing much you can do about it. If you live on the tenth floor of a block of flats and you have a baby in a pushchair, or you suffer from arthritis, then you are entirely dependent on the lift working. If the lift doesn't work then you're marooned ten storeys up and there is absolutely nothing you can do about it yourself, except walk up and down the stairs.

The more sophisticated and complicated our environment becomes the more numerous are the problems which develop. New machinery produces noise and pollutions of many other kinds.

There are increased risks of accidents occurring in heavily populated city areas where motor cars run in great profusion.

Stress and machines: Every development which adds to the complexity of modern life (and which admittedly may be designed to improve the quality of life) makes each one of us more and more dependent upon our neighbours and upon the others living in and working in the same local and national community. Ironically and tragically the machines and equipment designed to assist those who work on our behalf are now often so complicated and so sophisticated that it is the machines which are the principals in the provision of services and the human beings who are there to assist. This reversal of the traditional relationship between men and machines means that individuals are often so bored by the work that they do, and so deprived of any real sense of satisfaction, that they are likely to strike (and thereby create additional problems for thousands of fellow citizens) in order to establish their own identity. The better a city's facilities become the more likely it is that there will be problems, and the more certain it is that those problems will adversely affect large numbers of people.

All of this may be of little comfort next time you are stuck in a bus queue or stranded ten floors up without a lift or electricity but it does, I hope, illustrate just why living in a modern, twentieth-century city can be far more stressful than living in a primitive community. Problems you can solve yourself produce relatively little stress because there is only limited opportunity for frustration to develop. Problems that you cannot solve without the cooperation of others become immensely frustrating, and therefore immensely stressful, if the cooperation of those others is withheld for any reason.

The changing world

While writing this book I took time out one day to clear out some of the shelves in my study. I'm an inveterate book collector and from time to time the piles of books on the floor become too numerous and too high for me to move around without causing a series of minor avalanches. So I set about sorting through some of the books on the shelves in order to select volumes which could safely be moved into the cupboard under the stairs. I can never throw books out but I have steeled myself to move some that I am unlikely to need again into storage space.

What amazed me most on my purge along the shelves was the discovery that the majority of the textbooks that I had used when I was a medical student in the late 1960s were quite out of date. My guide to diseases of the stomach gave much space to the possible causes of duodenal ulcers but never mentioned stress or worry. My surgery textbook had been published when transplantation was a horticultural term. My psychiatry textbooks recommended brain surgery for disorders such as peptic ulceration and anxiety while drugs such as Valium and Librium were not mentioned at all. My pharmacology textbook gave Valium half a line but contained no mention of such modern and important drugs as cimetidine. The textbook which I used as a general introduction to medicine had nothing in it about endoscopy — now a routine investigative procedure. Just about the only textbooks which were still of any value were the anatomy texts. Things have changed so rapidly in the world of medicine that books which were considered accurate and up to date ten or fifteen years ago are now just so much worthless paper. Indeed, in some instances they are dangerous rather than useful.

If you stop and think about it for a minute or two you will quickly realize that it is not just in medicine or education that changes are taking place at a tremendous rate. In just about all aspects of life change is such a normal and readily accepted part of living that children who have grown up in the last few decades automatically assume that the things that they learn today will be just so much history by tomorrow. They expect and are accustomed to a world in which dolls, toys, clothes, records, books and television personalities move in and out of fashion with no more chance of permanence than snowflakes.

All this transience, novelty and diversity and changes in fashion have meant that the speed of living has changed and many people have found themselves in an almost permanent state of shock as they struggle to cope with the fact that aspects of life which they had formerly regarded as settled have now suddenly become as unstable and unpredictable as the world of haute couture. Inflation, economic revolutions, changes in measurement standards, the development and wider availability of computers — all these things have meant that life has become unbearably fast for some people. Some even find the fact that we live in a world dominated by disposables difficult to accept, and I have met many individuals who have been deeply worried by the thought of buying and then throwing away such items as pens, razors, lighters and torches.

It is not possible to halt change, of course, even though not all change can be regarded as progress. But by being aware of the fact that we live in an ever-changing society, by determining to maintain some certainty and structure in our own lives and by building up our own capacity for stress control we can all improve our chances of coping and surviving.

Boredom

Whenever I talk about stress and its causes in public I always find that there is a general assumption that people only really suffer from stress-induced illnesses when something is actually happening to them. Over the years most people seem to have come to regard stress as something only endured by harassed businessmen, overworked schoolteachers, housewives under pressure and others whose lives are conducted at a great pace.

Mention the word stress to most people and they will think of businessmen rushing from airport to airport, holding meetings in hotel corridors and nursing headaches, high blood pressure and stomach ulcers. Stress is something most of us associate with activity and according to our own personal experiences we may, when we think of stress, think of screaming children, bundles of wet nappies and broken-down washing machines or piles of un-typed letters, broken-down typewriters and angry employers.

All that is true enough, of course. It is a fact that an individual who is under excessive pressure will quite probably suffer from one or more stress-induced diseases. The businessman may have high blood pressure, the young mother under pressure may de-velop a migraine headache and the secretary who can no longer cope with her workload may end up with colitis.

But just as too much activity can cause stress so also can too little activity. And just as too much pressure can produce physical and mental damage so a lack of pressure can, paradoxically, produce exactly the same effect.

Having studied individuals under stress for several years now I'm convinced that boredom is indeed just about the largest single cause of stress in our modern society. I'll describe what I mean by discussing just three groups of people who illustrate exactly how a lack of activity and a lack of pressure can produce stress.

Housewives: Housewives probably make up the largest single group of individuals who are likely to be affected by boredom.

I realize that many thousands of women reading that sentence will probably react indignantly and quickly point out that they don't have time to be bored. They are far too busy making the beds, picking up bits of dirty laundry, preparing meals, washing up, cleaning the house, making sure that everyone has clean handkerchiefs and fresh socks, polishing the windows, and doing the thousand and one other chores which make up part of the housewife's daily duties.

Now, I am very happy to agree that all those activities will probably keep the average housewife busy. She'll undoubtedly be kept rushing round the house from the moment she gets up in the morning to the time when she flops down into an easy chair late at night. But I wonder how many of those scurrying house-wives would argue that they find their household chores satis-fying, or would claim that they actually enjoy washing up and polishing the floors? I wonder how many would claim that they get real satisfaction from throwing armfuls of dirty washing into the washing machine and then ironing what doesn't get chewed up by the spin dryer?

And how many would agree with me that most of these duties are dull, undemanding and boring?

Factory workers: The second group includes all those individuals who find their daily work less than satisfying. It is difficult to know just where to begin with this group because there are so many individuals who illustrate this particular point. But, for example, just consider the workforce in the average medium to large-sized car component factory.

On the shop floor the employee probably works alongside sophisticated pieces of machinery which do most of the difficult work and need to be fed with raw materials, given regular supplies of oil and maintained in good working order. Conveyor belts probably carry bits and pieces of partly completed machinery from one part of the factory floor to another, and the whole process of manufacture is geared to the needs and capabilities of the machines rather than of the men operating them. Men who might once have been regarded as skilled craftsmen are employed as simple machine minders, babysitting several thousand pounds' worth of highly complicated engineering and helping to produce small pieces of metal which have little or no significance to the individual concerned.

In the offices the white-collar workers are similarly subservient to machines. There, instead of machines which make individual items, there are computers and word processors which need to be fed with information and which, in turn, then produce recommendations and instructions. In the office, as on the factory floor, the machine is in charge.

Understandably anxious to compete with the production schedules met by their competitors, manufacturers install more and more machinery each year. And as those machines take over the most interesting and rewarding jobs, so the men employed in those factories are more likely to become bored by their work.

Machines were once used to assist men; today men are employed to assist and look after the machines. It is hardly surprising that in such well-organized factories where craftsmen are no longer employed and where job satisfaction is limited to the size of the pay packet strikes are common. Employees, whether they are working on the factory floor or in the offices, are frustrated by their lack of responsibility and the absence of any real sense of satisfaction in the work they do. The only chance they have to obtain some sense of satisfaction is by using their very presence as a weapon and by continually demanding shorter working hours and larger pay packets. The lack of identity and boredom which are common problems in such factories can only be relieved by striking.

Those in retirement: The third group of individuals who suffer a great deal from boredom includes those men and women who have retired and who no longer have any real duties or responsibilities. I regularly read about trade union officials claiming that their members should be allowed to retire early, and today it is by no means uncommon for men and women who are in their fifties to strap on their gold watches and hang up their working clothes. I always wonder if those trade union officials realize exactly what they are doing for their members when they campaign so ferociously for early retirement.

For although many individuals gain little enough satisfaction from their daily work they gain even less from their lives once they have put on their carpet slippers and left work for good. The man or woman who has retired will often consider him or herself to be in some way unwanted. There is no status in retirement and too few individuals have the capacity to carve out a meaningful life for themselves once they have left work for good.

Walk into an old peoples' home almost anywhere and look around you. You'll see row after row of sad, bored faces belonging to sad, bored old people who have nothing more exciting to do than complain about the quality of the gravy, moan about the unknown thief who took their favourite newspaper and mutter about the woman across the room who won't stop taking out her false teeth and cleaning them on her jumper. Boredom in old people's homes is the biggest threat, and yet it is something that men and women who keep working into their seventies, eighties and even nineties hardly ever know.

Those three examples aren't intended to be exhaustive by any means. Boredom is a problem that affects us all from time to time. Those three groups of people just happen to be the largest groups of individuals who are particularly likely to suffer stress as a result of their boredom.

The housewife who gets little satisfaction from her housework, who spends her time operating machines she doesn't understand, opening packets of instant food she doesn't like, and who lives on a housing estate where each family lives in an isolated brick and plaster cell will become disillusioned, depressed and bored.

The factory worker or office clerk who spends his time serving the needs of complex machines and who gets about as much job satisfaction as the machine itself will become disillusioned, depressed and bored.

And the man who has taken early retirement and who spends his time waiting for the day's television programmes to start and then complaining about them will also become disillusioned, depressed and bored.

For all these individuals it is the absence of pressure that has done the damage. Frustrated by the absence of any real test or trial for their talents they will become increasingly anxious as their awareness of the futility of their lives is matched by the feeling that somehow they are being cheated of success and satisfaction. Their boredom can lead to any one of the many disorders associated with stress.

2

Stress and Your Stomach

The intestinal or alimentary tract has the simple function of making food supplies available to the body and allowing the unwanted surplus to be discharged at the distant end of the tract. Since the whole system is basically a rather long tube it is quite reasonable to argue that food passing through the alimentary tract isn't actually inside the body at all until it has been absorbed through the intestinal wall at some point.

The digestive system: a brief anatomical introduction

An average sort of intestinal tract in an average sort of adult will be about 9 metres (30 feet) long and those 9 metres of gut are divided into a number of different parts. Each part of the intestinal tract has its own job to do.

The first part of the tube is called the oesophagus or gullet and this does nothing more than simply carry food directly from the mouth to the stomach. The stomach is dilated in comparison to the rest of the tract and looks a bit like one of those leather drinking bottles that nomads carry with them through the desert, or a small, slightly misshapen hot water bottle.

Within an hour or two after a meal has been eaten the stomach will be empty and the partly digested food will have been passed on through a fairly narrow orifice into the duodenum. The orifice which divides the stomach from the duodenum is guarded by a muscular valve called the pyloric sphincter which only opens when food is ready to move on out of the stomach.

By the time food gets into the duodenum it will have been attacked by the enzymes in both human saliva and the stomach's own digestive juices. In the duodenum it is met by bile which is produced by the liver and which helps digest fat, and by the enzymes which are produced by the pancreas to help break down

20

proteins, fats and starch.

The more or less completely digested food is now passed on into the small intestine where another set of enzymes completes the digestive process and where the resultant tiny particles are absorbed into the wall of the intestine.

By the time food has got to the end of the small intestine and is about to enter the part of the intestinal tract known as the large bowel it is little more than waste residue. Water is removed in the colon and mucus is secreted to help the stools pass easily along to the exit point; the actual digestive process has finished much earlier on.

How your stomach works

It is the job of the stomach to turn the vast variety of assorted foods that you drop into it into a moveable thick soup which can be passed on into the next part of the intestinal tract. The stomach is a vestibule to the rest of the intestinal tract and it is here that food is prepared for digestion. The stomach, it is important to understand, is not just a passive repository for food.

Your stomach helps digest food in two ways. First the cells of the stomach lining produce something like 3 litres of gastric juice every day. Of the different substances which make up these juices probably the most important is hydrochloric acid which is produced by the parietal cells. These exist in the stomach wall in a total population of something approaching a billion.

The power and effect of these juices is enhanced by the stomach's muscular wall which churns the food and the juices together before squirting the resultant soup-like mixture through a valve into the next part of the intestinal tract, the duodenum.

It is these two properties of the stomach which give it its power as a digestive force and there are a number of different factors which can influence both the production of acid and the activity of the stomach's muscular wall. Of these factors the two which are of the greatest significance in the normal stomach are the presence and absence of food.

A good deal of research has been done over the years to show just how food can trigger off the production of acid and the start of the digestive process. It is known that there are special cells in the stomach lining which can be triggered by the presence of food to produce a hormone which then stimulates the production of acid. It is known that when the stomach is stretched by the presence of food yet another complex reflex mechanism is triggered off in such a way as to produce more acid.

Pavlov's work: But important as this research is to physiologists it really doesn't take us very much further in practical terms than the work of Ivan Petrovich Pavlov, the Russian physiologist who, at the end of the nineteenth century, published his research work showing that the secretion of gastric juices starts as a result of a sequence of reflexes. Pavlov's work was mainly done on dogs and he began his work with an animal which had had two surgical operations. The first operation ensured that none of the food the animal ate actually reached its stomach. What happened was that the food simply fell out of an opening in the animal's throat instead of travelling down the oesophagus into the stomach. The second operation had made an opening in the animal's stomach so that gastric juices produced there could be collected.

Pavlov found that it wasn't necessary for the food to reach the stomach in order for the stomach to start secreting gastric juices. Even with the food falling out of the dog's neck the gastric juices were still being made in fairly large quantities.

It was then a fairly small step from this piece of research for Pavlov to discover that it wasn't necessary to feed the dog at all in order to stimulate the flow of gastric juices. The sight or smell of food was quite enough to get the gastric juices flowing.

And, finally, Pavlov found that he could produce reflexes in his experimental animals which didn't directly involve food at all. He found, for example, that he could stimulate the production of gastric juices by training dogs to associate the ringing of a bell with the availability of food. To begin with the dog would hear a bell ringing every time he was fed. And eventually the dog would assume that he was going to be fed when he heard the bell ringing.

Pavlov's work on conditioned reflexes had a great influence on many areas of medicine, but it was in the world of gastric physiology that he first made his mark.

Beaumont's work: Not that the Russian alone deserves all the credit for discovering the way in which food stimulates the stomach to secrete acid and begin the digestive process. An American army surgeon, William Beaumont, published work in 1833 which set the stage for much of Pavlov's work.

Beaumont's work was carried out on a Canadian halfbreed Indian called Alexis St Martin who had been accidentally wounded in a shooting accident and who had been left with an opening from his stomach onto his abdominal wall. The opening meant that Beaumont could easily study the way in which St Martin's stomach lining responded to various stimuli.

In some ways Beaumont's work was even more remarkable than that of Pavlov. Despite the fact that he began his work at an isolated military post in the forests of Michigan it was Beaumont who initially showed first, that one of the substances secreted by the stomach wall is hydrochloric acid and second, that food stimulates the secretion of gastric juices.

Cannon's work: The first work on hunger was done by an American too, but by an academic physiologist rather than an enthusiastic amateur. It was shortly after Pavlov had completed his canine studies in Russia that Walter Bradford Cannon, Professor of Physiology at Harvard Medical School for nearly the whole of the first half of the twentieth century, began to explore the nature of hunger pangs — those strange aches and gnawing feelings which seem to develop in the upper abdomen when the next meal is overdue.

With the aid of a brave student called Washburn who immortalized himself by learning to put up with having a rubber balloon in his stomach Cannon showed that when the human stomach is empty it contracts very powerfully. He showed, moreover, that it is the contraction of the stomach muscles which produces the sensation of hunger rather than the other way round.

All these men helped us to understand a little more just how the stomach works. And it was their research into the physiology of the normal stomach which has helped us to understand just what happens when things go wrong.

Why things go wrong

The normal functioning of the stomach (and indeed the duodenum) depends largely on there being a good, steady supply of the right sort of food. The stomach's only function is to prepare food for digestion and if there is too little or too much of the wrong sort of food then the stomach will begin to exhibit signs of distress.

Research workers are still not absolutely certain about precisely what other problems can cause damage to the stomach, but there is considerable evidence to suggest that drinking too much alcohol, smoking too many cigarettes and taking too many of the wrong sort of drugs will all produce damage to the digestive part of the intestinal tract by affecting the rate at which acid is produced, the speed and nature of the movements of the stomach's muscle wall, or the composition of the stomach lining.

There is also evidence which suggests that stomach and duodenal problems run in families and that men are more likely to get duodenal trouble than women.

But I believe that one of the most important factors in the development of stomach and duodenal problems is stress and although there is still no really conclusive evidence linking the development of stomach problems to pressure and worry I believe that the evidence which does exist is convincing. Indeed my own experience in practice suggests that the vast majority of stomach and duodenal problems are either caused directly by stress or are exacerbated by it.

24

Wolf's studies: One of the most dramatic studies to deal with the effect of stress on the stomach was done by Dr Stewart Wolf at about the same time that Pavlov was busy showing that dogs could be stimulated to salivate by the ringing of bells. Dr Wolf's work was largely done with the acid of a man who is simply known in the medical literature as Tom.

When he was a mere nine years old Tom made the mistake of stuffing some scalding hot clam chowder into his mouth. The scalding substance burned his oesophagus so badly that the tube became sealed and Tom could no longer eat by swallowing food in the normal way. An opening had to be made in his abdominal wall for food to be put directly into the stomach.

As the years went by Tom adapted very well to this problem and would chew his food in his mouth before spitting it into a funnel leading in through his abdominal wall. He adapted so well, in fact, that he deliberately kept away from doctors and it was more or less by chance that he and Dr Wolf ever met.

When they did meet, however, Dr Wolf and the senior doctor with whom he was working (who by one of those strange coincidences happened to be called Dr Wolff), arranged for Tom to be given a job as a hospital orderly. I think it's fair to say that they didn't do this entirely for philanthropic reasons for over the following years they wrote a number of scientific papers about Tom and his stomach, many of which are still regarded as of great significance. One of their most important discoveries was that the lining to Tom's stomach could be affected not just by food but also by stress.

They discovered that if Tom was annoyed or angry then his stomach wall cells produced huge amounts of unnecessary acid. The stomach lining seemed to produced extra amounts of acid in just the same way as the skin on his face would go bright red. And they also discovered that when Tom was angry and his stomach was producing too much acid they could reverse the whole process by helping to reassure and calm him.

From what we know about the way in which stress prepares the human body for action by pushing up the rate at which the circulatory system carries oxygen and food to the muscles it seems likely that the extra burst of acid is designed to ensure that any food supplies still awaiting the digestive problem will be prepared for absorption into the body as rapidly as possible.

Now although this piece of evidence seems fairly conclusive and although I and many other doctors have met and dealt with a huge number of patients whose stomach and duodenal problems can be linked directly to stress there still isn't any conclusive evidence that stress causes stomach problems.

And I'm afraid that there isn't likely to *ever* be any conclusive evidence linking stress and stomach disease for the very simple reason that it is *almost* impossible to measure the amount of stress that individuals are under and it *is* impossible to measure the amount of stress that individuals *were* under when they first started to develop their stomach problems.

Julie Young: Consider, for example, the case of Julie Young. She had married at the age of seventeen and very rapidly had two children. By the time she'd reached the grand old age of twenty she was an experienced, harassed and slightly world-weary mother. She lived in a small apartment on the nineteenth storey of a block of flats, and despite having to put up with all the usual problems associated with bringing up children while living so far above the ground she seemed to sail through life without too many problems.

When I first heard her complain of what sounded like fairly ordinary indigestion I initially blamed her diet which seemed to consist largely of a very unhealthy mixture of cigarettes, vermouth and chips. She seemed a calm, phlegmatic young woman and I had no reason to suspect that she was suffering from stress. I advised her to try and consume a slightly more nutritious diet and I prescribed an ordinary antacid for her to try.

That didn't really help very much, however, and a month later she was still suffering from exactly the same symptoms. Neither my dietary advice nor my prescription had helped.

We sat down together for half an hour and tried to work out

precisely what might be causing her symptoms. And eventually she confessed that what was really worrying her was a story she'd read in a national newspaper. The story had described how a small boy had fallen from the balcony of a flat on the fourteenth storey of a block in the north of England. Since reading the story she'd been absolutely terrified of leaving her children alone for more than a minute or two and she'd become absolutely obsessional about locking the door to their tiny balcony.

Her new habits had simply made things worse. Her husband was getting fed up with having to spend ages hunting for the key every time he wanted to go out onto the balcony to look at his tomato plants and Mrs Young herself was finding her obsession an enormous burden. On several occasions she'd found herself making her way back up to the nineteenth floor to check on the balcony door even though the children hadn't been left in the apartment.

It was only when she revealed these fears to me that I realized that her indigestion symptoms had very probably been produced by her stress and anxiety about the children. When I managed to help arrange for her balcony to be fitted with childproof railings the indigestion symptoms disappeared entirely.

Mrs Young illustrates very clearly the point I want to make. For even though I feel confident that her indigestion symptoms were produced by stress there is no way in which I can *prove* the connection conclusively. There is strong circumstantial evidence in that the pains were present when she was worrying and they disappeared when she stopped worrying. But that doesn't provide solid scientific proof that stress caused damage to her stomach.

John Elder: The case of Mr John Elder also illustrates this same point. For five years Mr Elder had driven a bus on a busy city route and for most of that time he had been accompanied on his journeys by a conductor. Mr Elder had been responsible for driving the bus and for making sure that the company's schedules were kept, and conductor's job was to ensure that each passenger paid the correct fare.

Mr Elder's problems arose when the company decided to save some money by introducing a fleet of pay-as-you-enter buses. For Mr Elder this was a very significant change. Instead of simply having to cope with driving his bus through the busy city traffic, he now also had the responsibility of taking money from would-be passengers and providing them with tickets.

He found that this was by no means as easy a task as it sounds. One major problem was that many of the people who got onto the bus didn't have the correct change and would argue angrily when he pointed to the notice informing would-be passengers that only people carrying the right coins would be allowed to ride on the bus. On several occasions Mr Elder found himself being threatened and eventually he gave up arguing with passengers and simply provided the change if it was required. This in turn made him unpopular with the other drivers who were sticking rigidly to the regulations.

After two weeks of this Mr Elder came to my surgery complaining of stomach pains. He was obviously very distressed and, in addition to giving him a supply of antacid tablets designed to relieve the immediate discomfort, I provided him with a sick note for work, suggesting that he should take at least a fortnight off duty.

When, two weeks later, Mr Elder returned to the surgery he seemed a different man. He looked very much better and said he felt much improved. He was eager to get back to work, so I provided him with a certificate stating that he was fit to start driving his bus again.

That, unfortunately, was when his problems began again. Within three days of starting back to work and finding himself besieged by angry passengers Mr Elder was back in my consulting room pleading for more antacid tablets and another sick note.

Now once again I think that it is entirely reasonable to assume that the stress of driving a pay-as-you-enter bus had caused Mr Elder's stomach symptoms. The symptoms had, after all, developed within a few days of his starting the new job, they had disappeared when he'd stayed away from work, and they had returned when he'd gone back to work.

But although it is a reasonable assumption, it is nothing more than that. Once again the evidence is purely circumstantial. A cynical scientist might, for example, argue that Mr Elder simply didn't like going to work and that accordingly he was inventing the symptoms of which he complained. He might also argue that Mr Elder's symptoms were a result of the fact that when at work he ate sandwiches; or that the symptoms had been produced by the fact that Mr Elder sat in the cab all the time or breathed in carbon monoxide fumes from a faulty exhaust.

I may well be convinced that Mr Elder's stomach symptoms were a result of his stress at work, but there is no way in which I can *prove* that the association exists.

Establishing a strict and formal relationship between stress and stomach problems is made even more difficult by the fact that individuals who are under stress are very often also the same sort of people who drink too much alcohol, smoke too much and eat irregularly or too quickly. (I believe that stress is very often the underlying cause for many of these habits too but I can't prove that either.)

How does stress cause symptoms?

Built into your body there is a remarkable series of defence mechanisms designed to enable you to deal with threats and dangers as quickly and as effectively as possible. The aim of these mechanisms is simply to enable you to defend yourself and to survive whatever the threat may be — fight or flight.

These defence mechanisms have been developed and improved over very many centuries and they are primarily designed to cope with immediate problems requiring urgent action. If, for example, you're about to be attacked by a man-eating sabre-tooth tiger then your body will automatically prepare for the attack.

29

Information about the impending attack is fed immediately into your central nervous system and the pituitary gland deep inside your skull produces a hormone called adrenocortico-trophic hormone (ACTH) which is designed specifically to stimulate the adrenal glands. The adrenal glands in turn then produce two sets of hormones: adrenaline and steroids. These hormones from the adrenal gland have an effect throughout the body. They increase the blood pressure, close down the superficial blood vessels, improve the blood supply to the muscles, tense the muscles and even make your hairs stand on end. And they increase the flow of acid into your stomach.

All these actions have a purpose. The blood pressure goes up and the heart rate increases so that your muscles and brain have the best possible supply of nutrients. Your muscles tense so that you are ready to spring into action. Your superficial blood vessels constrict so that the amount of blood circulating through the skin is kept to a minimum. This not only ensures that there is a good supply to the essential organs, but it also limits the amount of blood that would be lost if you are bitten by the tiger. Your hairs stand on end to try and make you look larger. The extra acid that flows into your stomach is designed to turn any food there into digestible form just as soon as possible. Your body needs all the energy supply it can get its glands on!

Now if you really are being threatened by a sabre-tooth tiger all these actions are a tremendous help, of course. Your body will be that much better able to cope as a result of all these changes. You'll be able to run faster, jump higher and punch harder. You'll be much more likely to survive the attack thanks to the flood of hormones that have swept through your body.

But unfortunately the human body cannot differentiate between situations, and it has not yet learned to adapt to our modern way of life in which problems are not usually so easily solved by simple physical methods.

What happens, therefore, is that when you are threatened with some problem such as redundancy or a retirement that you don't really want to take, your body reacts in exactly the same way that it would have reacted to that sabre-toothed tiger. There are changes in your cardiovascular system and your blood pressure rises. There is a continuing flood of acid into your stomach and you may also develop a peptic ulcer as a souvenir of the experience.

Whereas the confrontation with the tiger would have been over one way or another quite quickly, the state of unemployment (or whatever stress it is that you are facing) may well go on for weeks, months or even years. And the result of that is that your body's own defence system, designed to help you cope more effectively with danger, is in fact likely to produce problems of its own.

The human body is still designed for operation in environments where action must be taken quickly and where stimuli are unlikely to go on for too long. It has not yet adapted properly to modern life where stimuli *are* likely to persist and where there is often no escape from those stimuli.

What types of stomach problems are there?

It is impossible in a book of this kind to describe all the different kinds of stomach problems that can exist. Any introductory gastroenterology textbook contains scores of pages describing no more than the most rudimentary details about the disorders which can affect the oesophagus, stomach and duodenum. A fully comprehensive gastroenterology textbook would need hundreds of pages to cover the same area.

Nor is it possible to classify only the less serious stomach problems or the ones which have a temporary effect. The truth is that it is often exceedingly difficult to come to a specific decision about the precise nature of any particular stomach problem without conducting investigations which require professional help and sophisticated equipment. And since the purpose of this book is not to enable you to make a diagnosis but to help you restrict the effects of stress on your stomach, and thereby limit your symptoms, any attempt to describe or classify stomach problems

31

would be irrelevant.

What I have done in this section is to describe some of the words most commonly used by people who complain of stomach problems and to offer some simple explanations designed to help provide a guide to the differences which exist. All the problems described here can have physical causes but can also be a direct result of too much stress.

Indigestion: This isn't a word that doctors use a great deal when describing stomach problems because it is a particularly vague sort of word which doesn't really mean anything definite. In literal terms the word indigestion simply means that there has been a failure of digestion and so it can theoretically refer to a small intestine problem as well as a stomach problem.

In practice, the word is used to describe the sort of symptoms which occur when a meal is eaten too quickly or after an unusually spicy or fatty meal.

Sufferers usually complain of some pain in the centre of the chest and they may also feel slightly bloated. It's common for indigestion sufferers to complain of excessive wind and nausea. Occasionally an indigestion sufferer will actually vomit. Very few people who have indigestion will be interested in food for the pain tends to be accompanied by a full feeling and a loss of appetite.

Indigestion can be caused by smoking too much, by drinking too much alcohol or by taking too much tea or coffee. Other drugs, such as aspirin, can also cause indigestion.

However, although these specific causes are significant many of the individuals who suffer from indigestion do so directly as a result of stress.

Dyspepsia: There is no difference between dyspepsia and indigestion.

Heartburn: Under normal circumstances the acid mixture that helps to digest food within the stomach is kept away from the

32

oesophagus by a sphincter which allows food to travel down into the stomach but doesn't allow food and acid to travel upwards into the gullet. If the sphincter which usually divides the oesophagus from the stomach in this way doesn't do its job properly acid can sometimes splash upwards and irritate the oesophageal mucosa. The word 'heartburn' is very descriptive. Even when the sphincter is in good working condition acid can irritate the oesophagus when you lie down or bend over. Naturally enough, therefore, individuals who have a weak sphincter at that point will find that they suffer far more when they are lying flat or bending over than they do when they are standing up straight.

Despite the fact that heartburn can have a solid physical cause there are many individuals who suffer from this symptom purely as a result of stress.

Gastritis: Gastritis is an inflammation of the stomach that can be produced by alcohol, by the consumption of a foodstuff to which you are allergic, by a virus infection or by any one of a number of other mechanisms which are not yet properly understood. There are some specific changes in the stomach mucosa when gastritis is present, but in practice it is virtually impossible to differentiate clinically between dyspepsia, gastritis and peptic ulcers without undergoing specific investigations such as a barium meal examination or an endoscopy.

Peptic ulcer: The term peptic ulcer, gastric ulcer and duodenal ulcer are often used as though they are completely interchangeable. In fact, however, there are differences. A *peptic* ulcer is simply any ulcer in the upper part of the intestinal tract. The word 'peptic' is used as a synonym for digestion. A *gastric* ulcer, however, is one that is found in the stomach, while a *duodenal* ulcer is one that is found in the duodenum. The phrase peptic ulceration can be used to describe both a stomach ulcer *or* a duodenal ulcer.

Ulcers of all kinds result from an imbalance between the power of the secretions produced by the stomach and the resistance of the lining of the part of the intestine concerned.

Gastric ulcer: We still really don't know precisely what causes a gastric ulcer or why the acid suddenly starts to eat away at the stomach lining to produce an ulcer cavity. What we do know is that although individuals who have gastric ulcers don't seem to be producing more acid than other people they do have a weaker stomach lining.

There is also evidence that the stomach lining or mucosa can be damaged by a number of different factors — tobacco, alcohol and fats, for example. This explains why individuals who have gastric ulcers will usually get better quicker if they cut out cigarettes and alcohol and if they steer away from fatty foods as much as possible.

Gastric ulcer pain is usually localized to the epigastrium, a central point about half way between the chin and the umbilicus, and eating usually makes it worse. Unlike duodenal ulcer pain gastric ulcer pain doesn't usually go away once it has started. To deal with a gastric ulcer it is usually necessary either to increase the resistance of the mucosa or to decrease the production of stomach acid.

Duodenal ulcer: Scientists still have not yet decided precisely how duodenal ulcers develop, but it is widely believed that they result from some imbalance between the power of the stomach's acid secretions to attack and the ability of the duodenal lining to resist the attack. It is a fine balance and one that can fairly easily be tipped one way or the other.

The most important symptom of a duodenal ulcer is usually pain, and indeed this is often the only symptom that occurs. The pain is usually localized in the epigastrium, and, unlike gastric ulcers, eating usually helps relieve the pain. People who have duodenal ulcers will often wake up at night and sneak downstairs to get a glass of milk and a biscuit.

The other characteristic factor of the pain that people get with duodenal ulceration is that it tends to disappear for weeks or even months at a time for no very apparent reason. Suddenly, just when you thought it had gone away for ever back it comes with a bang!

To deal with a duodenal ulcer it is usually necessary to either increase the resistance of the mucosa or decrease the production of stomach acid.

Nausea: This is by no means a symptom caused exclusively by the consumption of foodstuffs which upset the system. Nausea and vomiting can also be a sign of stress and distress. The phrase 'you make me sick' is well established as a colloquialism, and many people feel sick or actually vomit when confronted by a gory sight. Nausea and vomiting are usually symptoms of acute stress rather than chronic, long-lasting anxiety.

Wind: The normal gastrointestinal tract is said to contain between 100 and 200 millilitres of gas under normal circumstances. During an ordinary sort of day a normal individual will often produce 1 to 2 litres of gas. It is, therefore, quite obvious that there must be a tendency for wind to pass out of the gastrointestinal tract at one end or the other.

Wind is produced within the gastrointestinal tract as food is digested, and some foods are more likely than others to result in the production of large quantities of wind. Brussels sprouts and cabbage are fairly widely recognized as offending vegetables and beans, of course, have a tremendous reputation in this respect.

It is, however, important to understand that not all of the wind in the gastrointestinal tract is a result of the normal digestive process. Some of the wind that causes such embarrassing noises gets into the intestinal tract in the same way that food gets in: it is swallowed. People who chew gum, smoke cigarettes or eat too quickly will often swallow air as will those individuals who gulp in air as a nervous habit.

3

The Medical Approach

Although this is basically a self-help book I believe that anyone who has persistent or recurrent stomach symptoms should seek medical advice before trying to solve their problems themselves. I say this not only because it is often extremely difficult to differentiate between the different types of stomach disorder, but because it is also sometimes very difficult to differentiate between stomach problems and other diseases.

When should you see your doctor?

It is, for example, often extremely tricky to differentiate between angina, which is an early warning sign of heart trouble, and indigestion which is a warning sign of stomach trouble. Let me give two examples to explain what I mean.

Mr Kennedy: Mr Kennedy lived with his wife in a small terraced house where they had in fact spent the whole of their married life together. It was rather an old-fashioned house and since Mrs Kennedy didn't like the idea of having workmen wandering through knocking out bricks and generally creating havoc they didn't have any electricity or an indoor lavatory. Everyone else in the terrace had both but the Kennedys remained resolutely opposed to any such technical advances.

They both managed quite well without these conveniences and although I was their family doctor I only saw them very occasionally. They were proud, independent and generally quite healthy.

It was Mr Kennedy who came to see me to ask for a bottle of indigestion medicine. He explained that every night when he went to the lavatory after his evening meal he had a pain in his chest. He was quite convinced that the pain was caused by indigestion, but although he'd tried adjusting his eating habits he hadn't managed to eliminate the discomfort.

When I talked to him I discovered that the pain had only begun to bother him during the winter months and that it had been worst during a particularly cold spell when snow had remained on the ground for ten days or so. More questioning told me that he never had any indigestion at any other time of day, and that he never got the pain unless he went out of doors.

Mr Kennedy had made a dangerous and incorrect assumption in guessing that his pain was due to indigestion. In fact it was an angina pain produced by his habit of taking exercise during the colder evening hours. It is well known that heart pain is exacerbated by cold weather since the cold has a constrictive effect on the blood vessels.

Once the diagnosis had been made I was able to offer useful and constructive advice. In fact it was *very* constructive advice because I suggested that they have an indoor lavatory built at long last. When they finally did so the chest pains stopped.

That story ended happily, but it could easily have ended quite differently. If Mr Kennedy had continued to regard his pain as nothing more than indigestion, and had done nothing about it, he could quite well have had a heart attack one evening on his way to the lavatory.

Mr Blundell: The other patient I want to describe, Mr Blundell, worked in a car factory as a machine operator. He came to see me in quite a state because he was totally convinced that he was getting heart pains.

Every morning he drove his car part of the way to the factory where he worked but because of the congestion in the works car park he had recently got into the habit of leaving his car in the driveway of a friend's house. The driveway was about half a mile from the factory but Mr Blundell found it quicker to walk that last half a mile than to park his car and then make his way into the factory.

He was developing his pains every morning as he began his

walk to the factory, and he explained to me that he had put the pains down to heart trouble for the simple reason that he could think of no other possible explanation. In fact when I examined him I could find absolutely nothing wrong. His heart was in perfect condition, his arteries seemed perfectly patent and his blood pressure was quite normal for a man of his age.

The real explanation for Mr Blundell's pain was very simple. When he parked his car in the driveway at the friend's house each day Mr Blundell popped his head into the kitchen to say 'hello'. And every day when he did that he had a bacon sandwich popped into his mouth. He didn't like refusing and he didn't like walking along the road with a bacon sandwich in his hand so he scoffed the sandwich rather hurriedly. And that gave him indigestion.

Tests: Differentiating between angina and indigestion, between indigestion and peptic ulceration, between gastritis and gastric carcinoma and between simple heartburn and serious oesophageal disease requires professional assistance. I believe that anyone who has any of the stomach symptoms I've described for more than five days or who suffers from recurrent attacks of any symptom needs medical advice.

Once your family doctor has listened to your story he will be able to make a decision about whether or not further investigations are necessary. He may, for example, decide that you need to have a barium meal examination. This commonly performed test relies on the fact that barium that has been swallowed can be seen quite clearly on an X-ray outlining the inner walls of the stomach and duodenum. If there are any abnormalities in the stomach or duodenum lining the radiologist who studies the X-ray film will be able to spot them straight away. Alternatively, your doctor may decide to refer you to a local specialist for endoscopy. In this test a flexible tube is pushed down the oesophagus and into the stomach. Through the tube the viewer can see inside the stomach and duodenum and may even be able to take photographs.

If any of the tests that are done suggest that there is any need for additional specialist advice or for surgical intervention then your doctor will obviously make the necessary arrangements. In the majority of cases, however, whether the tests are positive or negative, your doctor will probably feel able to offer treatment without specialist help. Whatever treatment he recommends there will be no contraindication to your initiating your own programme of stress control, for whatever the nature of your stomach problem stress will make it worse and stress control will help to make it better.

Is there a value in bedrest?

It used to be said that individuals with stomach problems would get better quicker if they rested in bed for days at a time. I don't think that there was ever any real evidence that bedrest actually helped ease an ulcer or accelerated the natural healing process, and in fact I rather suspect that many individuals who were forced to rest in bed by dictatorial physicians may well have suffered more stress than if they had been allowed to remain mobile.

I remember that when I was working in a hospital some years ago one of the consultants used to insist that his patients with stomach disorders should remain in bed for at least seven days and preferably ten days. He also used to insist that no patients should be allowed access to the telephone on the grounds that any aggravation or outside pressure would simply make things worse.

I lost faith in this particular theory when we had a patient in hospital who earned his living writing racing tips for one of the evening newspapers. He had acquired his peptic ulcer as a result of a lifetime of financial problems, and when he was told that he couldn't use the telephone to send his racing tips in to his office, and that he had to stay in bed isolated from the television, the radio and the visitors who could bring him news of all the latest betting he got worse rather than better. Being stuck in bed and isolated from the outside world meant that he lost his job. The result of that was that his financial problems got worse. And so did his peptic ulcer.

So it isn't bedrest that helps — it's stress control.

The use of antacids

I don't suppose that there are many patients around who have never tried a spoonful of the traditional white medicine that is used to help counteract so many stomach problems.

The theory is simple enough: by taking an antacid you are putting something into your stomach that is designed to help counteract the powerful and potentially damaging effect of the hydrochloric acid produced in the stomach. As it is the hydrochloric acid that does much of the damage the hope is that the antacid will prevent this damage occurring.

There are several things about antacids that are worth remembering.

1. Antacids are available as liquids, powders and tablets. Although liquids and powders usually work better than tablets (which often need to be chewed or sucked very thoroughly) they're far less convenient. It is much easier to carry tablets around in your pocket, handbag or car glove compartment. A bottle of tablets carried with you will do a lot more good than a bottle of medicine at home in the bathroom cabinet.

2. The antacids that doctors prescribe are no different to the antacids that can be bought over the counter without a prescription.

3. Sodium bicarbonate (baking soda) is a good 'emergency' antacid. It is not suitable for long-term treatment because of the side-effects that can follow its prolonged use, but it is a useful standby since it can be used to provide relief on a Saturday night long after all the chemists' shops have shut.

4. If taken in relatively small quantities antacids will only help relieve symptoms, but there is now some evidence to support the view that if they are taken in much larger quantities antacids can

40

actually help heal an ulcer. Most people who use antacids take them in quantities which are far too modest. To gain full benefit from antacid you probably need to take 30 millilitres of a mixture seven times a day. However, if you intend using an antacid in such large quantities then you should check with your doctor first. There is no need to seek medical advice before using antacids to obtain temporary relief, but you should not use them persistently without an investigation to assess the nature of the damage in your stomach.

5. Antacids can, like other medicines, have side-effects. There is no medicine available that has useful properties but no side-effects. The two commonest side-effects with antacids are diarrhoea and constipation. Magnesium salts usually cause diarrhoea while aluminium salts tend to cause constipation. To overcome these problems many manufacturers sell mixtures of both aluminium salt and magnesium compound.

6. Some antacid mixtures also contain dimethicone or dimethyl-polysiloxane. These are substances which help small bubbles of air coalesce to form larger bubbles. The larger bubbles then get out of the stomach far more readily than the smaller bubbles. Antacid mixtures that contain one of these additional substances, therefore, are particularly suitable for individuals who have a lot of wind that they cannot get rid of.

Other medical therapies

Carbenoxolone: This is a form of synthetic liquorice and although the way it works is still something of a mystery it is thought to help relieve symptoms and accelerate healing by increasing the resistance of the stomach lining to the acid. It may also increase the production of mucus within the stomach.

The main side-effect with this drug includes the retention of salt and water and a consequent effect on the blood pressure. A patient who is taking carbenoxolone should, therefore, have his blood pressure and weight checked regularly and if treatment continues for more than a month or so blood tests are a sensible idea.

Cimetidine and ranitidine: Although it was only introduced into clinical practice in 1976 cimetidine has been the subject of nearly 4,000 scientific publications and is said to have been used in over 15 million patients. Some researchers believe that it is very effective in the treatment of existing peptic ulcers. There are papers which show that 50 percent of peptic ulcers can be expected to heal within three weeks, with 90 percent healing within six weeks.

Cimetidine is believed to work by inhibiting the production of acid and there is now another drug, ranitidine which seems to have a similar effect. Some observers claim that ranitidine is as effective as cimetidine but has fewer side effects and is less likely to interact with other prescribed drugs. Of all the drugs commonly available for the treatment of peptic ulceration these are probably the ones most likely to produce a cure.

Anticholinergics: These compounds used to be popularly prescribed for the treatment of stomach problems but I don't know of any real evidence that they work. They are not widely used today because they produce a number of side-effects, including drowsiness, dry mouth and blurred vision.

Bismuth salts: Although researchers do not yet really know why it works there is some evidence to suggest that a substance called tripotassium dicitrate bismuthate can help heal peptic ulcers. The main disadvantage with this treatment is that the available liquid preparation has a very unpleasant smell. The newly available tablet form of this drug is usually more acceptable.

Surgery: This is only ever contemplated when a patient has undergone a full series of investigations and it has been shown that there is some genuine peptic ulceration present. The type of operation selected will vary according to the site of the ulcer and the severity of the individual's condition.

If the ulcer is in the stomach (and therefore known as a gastric ulcer) the most popular operation is still the Billroth I anastomosis. This procedure is named after the surgeon who first performed the operation towards the end of the nineteenth century, and consists of removing completely the part of the stomach that contains the ulcer. The procedure is also called partial gastrectomy.

If the ulcer is in the duodenum the surgeon will often try cutting the vagus nerve since this is known to be the pathway along which acid-producing stimuli pass into the stomach wall. The theory is that if the vagus nerve is cut fewer stimuli will reach the stomach and less acid will be produced there. The efficiency of the operation depends largely upon the efficiency of the surgeon in his attempts to cut the vagus nerve.

Tranquillizers: Because there is known to be a very close relationship between stomach problems and stress some doctors treat patients with disorders of this kind with tranquillizers. The aim is simply to relax the individual patient and to increase his capacity to put up with stresses and strains.

Unfortunately, there are a number of side-effects known to be associated with the use of tranquillizers. It is now recognized that if these drugs are taken for more than a few weeks addiction and habituation can develop. Many patients have reported that they have had considerable difficulty in weaning themselves off tranquillizers. Other patients have complained that because of their sedative effect tranquillizers have damaged the quality of their lives.

My own feeling is that tranquillizers should only be used for *very* short periods of time since they only offer a temporary solution. If you are suffering from stomach symptoms then your problem is likely to be a long-term one unless you make a creative effort either to minimize your exposure to stress or to enhance your own ability to withstand stress.

Relaxation therapy: If you are very fortunate your doctor will have the time to spend teaching you how to relax. If he is prepared to help you in this way then you should be able to build up your resistance to stress speedily and effectively and you should, therefore, be able to minimize the extent to which you suffer from stomach problems in the future.

Of course, if your doctor *does* have the time to spend teaching you how to cope with stress yourself then it is unlikely that you will have bought this book!

The limitations of medical treatment

The majority of medical and surgical treatments offered by doctors and surgeons to people suffering from stomach problems are designed to relieve their symptoms and cure their existing stomach troubles.

There is after all a very strong tradition within the medical profession that it is a doctor's job to make a specific diagnosis and to then offer a specific solution. This ancient philosophy means that there is a tendency for practitioners to treat patients with indigestion or peptic ulcers with specific remedies for indigestion or peptic ulcers. Since most doctors have practice commitments which are so huge that any consultation lasting more than a few minutes is likely to cause problems of its own it is hardly surprising that the symptom gets treated and the cause remains undiscovered; or to put it more accurately, the disease gets treated and the cause of the disease remains free to do damage again.

This link between expediency and the traditional medical approach is supported and strengthened by the widely held feeling that anything offered as a solution which cannot be sugarcoated, put into a bottle and prescribed is at best dubious and at the very worst highly unprofessional. Although the hazards associated with tranquillizers are now well recognized, and the advantages associated with relaxation therapy and stress control widely accepted, there are still more medical practitioners prescribing tranquillizers than there are recommending relaxation.

To all that we must also add the fact that for strong historical reasons the relationship between doctors and patients is based very much on single consultations. Patients usually go to see doctors when they are ill and doctors usually get paid for offering advice and treatments. Only in some parts of ancient China were doctors paid to keep their patients well. With the relationship so strongly based on the individual consultation it is perhaps hardly surprising that many modern doctors still regard their prime function as the treatment of existing disease rather than the prevention of potential disorders.

My own feeling is that if this archaic attitude could be discarded, and doctors convinced that a medical approach which contained stronger elements of prevention than treatment was acceptable, then more members of the medical profession could perhaps be encouraged to offer their patients advice on how best to deal with pressures and pains without developing ulcers, indigestion and other problems.

Meanwhile, until that time comes I recommend that patients should themselves think in terms of prevention rather than treatment, of helping themselves rather than relying on medical aid, and should aim for a long-term cure rather than a short-term solution.

4

What You Should Do

In most of the medical advice books I've written I've tried to
teach readers how best to cope with their own problems without
seeking medical advice. This subject is, however, rather exceptional in that it is often extremely difficult for the individual who
has the symptoms to know precisely how serious the problem is. I
have known some patients with quite severe peptic ulceration
complain of nothing more than intermittent mild pain, while on
the other hand I have also known patients complain of very bad
pain when subsequent investigations have shown no evidence
whatsoever of there being any physical signs of damage.

And I think it is also worth repeating the point that it is by no
means always easy to be certain about the diagnosis when dealing
with chest pain. In all sorts of patients, but particularly in men in
their thirties, forties and fifties, early heart pain may occasionally
mimic bad indigestion and a mistaken diagnosis at this stage can
prove fatal.

Be sure about the diagnosis: use your doctor

I suggest that you should visit your doctor if you have had any
recurring pains which you suspect might be due to stomach problems, or if you have any pain which persists for more than five
days. Obviously you'll visit your doctor anyway if you vomit up
blood, if you have severe pain or if you notice any other symptom
such as weight or appetite loss.

One of the most important things that your doctor can do is to
confirm the diagnosis or exclude any serious pathology. But most
doctors will also offer some form of treatment and you will probably leave the surgery with a prescription for one of the drugs
described in chapter 3.

All of these treatments will help relieve your symptoms and

they may even temporarily speed up the natural healing process. But what you must remember is that chewing antacid tablets to help cure indigestion can only offer a short-term solution. If your car has a leaky radiator hose you can solve the problem temporarily by pouring more water into the radiator. This will not, however, provide a lasting answer to your problem. If you have a leak in the roof you can disguise the damp patch on the bedroom ceiling by repapering every week, but that won't stop the damp patch reappearing the next time it rains.

Your stomach problems may well be relieved temporarily by the use of antacids, cimetidine or one of the other useful products. But if the *cause* of your problem remains undisturbed then your symptoms will eventually recur.

Look after your stomach

Most of us have a weak point. Some people get headaches when they are under pressure. Others get asthma, heart pains, diarrhoea or skin rashes. The human body, like most complex pieces of machinery doesn't all go wrong at once. There is usually one part that is weaker than the rest. And if you are a regular sufferer from indigestion, ulcer pains or other stomach symptoms then the chances are that your stomach is your weak point.

It is, therefore, important that you do what you can to look after your stomach and keep it healthy. To begin with it is a good idea to learn to listen to your stomach and to get into the habit of eating when you are hungry rather than just because the clock tells you that it is time to eat. Few people realize that we do in fact all have an appetite control centre which is designed to control our eating habits quite accurately.

A study published in the *American Journal of Diseases of Children* some years ago showed that when newly weaned infants just a few months old were allowed to choose what they ate from a range of simple, natural foods they selected balanced diets which were just as good in nutritional value as the carefully balanced ideal diets worked out by nutritional experts.

47

Another study published in the *Journal of the American Dental Association* showed that young children automatically choose foods that enable them to avoid digestive upsets and constipation. A third study, done on soldiers during the Second World War, showed that when allowed access to unlimited supplies of food, troops ate what their bodies needed according to the outside temperature and that they automatically chose an ideal mixture of protein, fat and carbohydrate.

Unfortunately, most of us have lost the art of listening to our own bodies and we tend to eat three meals a day whether we are hungry or not, stuffing our bodies with food not because we need it but because the clock says it is time to eat. In practice the stomach does not adapt well to huge meals at lengthy intervals and it can cope far more effectively with smaller meals taken at shorter intervals.

We've also lost the art of knowing when we've had enough to eat, and most of us make the mistake of always finishing the food on our plates because we've been trained that wasting food is wrong. Again what is happening is that the appetite control centre is being ignored and food is being eaten in the remarkable belief that unwanted food is better off inside the body than in the dustbin.

Your stomach will be much healthier (and far less likely to succumb to stress) if you re-establish control of your appetite control centre by eating when you feel hungry, stopping when you feel full and nibbling smaller meals more frequently rather than stuffing yourself with large meals occasionally.

Rules for better eating habits: In addition you can do much to minimize the damage that your eating habits do to your stomach by following these simple rules.

1. Eat slowly. People often stuff food into their mouths at an unbelievable rate when they are under stress. A medical friend of mine used to be spooning up the last smear of custard while the rest of us were still finishing our soup. He always had indigestion afterwards and had to sit for half an hour to allow the pain to disappear.

2.   Don't try eating while you're reading or watching the television. A little mild and gentle conversation probably won't do much harm but you should concentrate as much as you can when you're eating. Only by concentrating on what you are doing will you become able to tell when your stomach is talking to you. And if you listen it *will* talk to you, and tell you when you're eating something that is going to upset you, or eating too much.

3.   Try and put small forkfuls into your mouth. Stuff huge amounts of food onto your fork and you'll end up failing to chew your food properly. Chewing is an essential part of the digestive process and the saliva in your mouth contains enzymes which help prepare your food for the secretions produced by the stomach.

4.   Try to taste each mouthful of food that you eat. That way you're far less likely to eat unnecessarily or too quickly.

5.   If you are a fast eater put down your knife and fork between mouthfuls. That will slow you down very effectively.

6.   Don't let other people push you into eating when you aren't hungry or when you don't want a second helping. And do be prepared to leave food on the side of your plate if you've had enough to eat.

7.   Remember that regular meals are better for you than irregular meals. By eating regularly you'll be helping to mop up some of the acid in your stomach. If you eat irregularly the acid in your stomach will have nothing to get its teeth into.

8.   When you've finished a meal have a short rest. Give your stomach time to do its job before you start chasing around again.

9.   Try to find out what sort of foods upset your stomach most — and avoid them. Different people are badly affected by different foods, so it is impossible to offer a comprehensive list of foods to avoid but if you do have a 'weak' stomach it is likely that any of the foods on the list below will exacerbate your symptoms:

All fried foods
Strong tea or coffee
Fizzy drinks
Alcohol
Fatty foods
Spicy foods
Pickles, curry, peppers, mustard
Broad beans, brussels sprouts, radishes and cucumber
Unripe fruit
Very hot or very cold foods
Coarse bread, biscuits or cereals
Nuts or dried fruit
Any tough food (meat for example) that can't be chewed easily

You do *not* have to avoid all these foods if you have stomach symptoms. But do be aware that these foods can cause problems. The important thing is to find out which foods upset *you* and avoid them. Do remember that *when* and *how* you eat probably affects your stomach more than *what* you eat.

Give up smoking

We don't know very much about the ways in which peptic ulcers develop but we do know that tobacco smoke irritates the lining of the stomach and makes it more vulnerable to attack by acid. All stomach sufferers will, therefore, suffer far less if they can give up smoking.

There are a great many different methods around which have been advocated as being suitable for helping smokers to kick the habit. By and large any method that works is a good one. If, however, you've tried to give up smoking in the past and failed you might find it helpful to try one of the following techniques.

1.   Keep a daily note of just how much money you spend on cigarettes or tobacco. It is astonishing to see just how quickly the sums of money mount up. If you're cutting down on cigarettes keep another record of the amount of money that you've man-

aged to save. You can reward yourself by planning to buy something you'd really like with the money that would otherwise have gone up in smoke.

2. Try to make your cigarette buying as complicated as possible. Buy a different brand of cigarette every day, for example, or buy them from a different shop every day. Never buy more than one packet at once. Buy in packets of ten.

3. If you find the prospect of cutting out cigarettes in one brave move too much to contemplate then try preparing a plan whereby you have to cut out your smoking habit in easy stages.

You might find that it helps if you begin by telling yourself that you won't smoke during mealtimes. Or that you won't smoke at work. Or that you won't smoke while watching television. This trick means that you don't have to produce such an enormous amount of willpower in order to reduce your smoking. After you've cut out smoking in the car, smoking on the train or smoking in the street you can make up your mind that you will only smoke when you aren't doing anything else at all.

A variation on this technique is to cut out your smoking room by room. Start by cutting out smoking in the bedroom and the bathroom. Just tell yourself that you'll never smoke in those rooms again. And then add other rooms to your list as the days go by. Within a week you'll find yourself standing on the doorstep smoking furtive cigarettes. At that point most people find giving up the cigarettes a positive relief.

I can't leave the subject of smoking without pointing out that there is a strong link between stress and cigarettes. Many smokers will confirm that their consumption of cigarettes goes up when they are stressed or worried and that the number of cigarettes they smoke falls when they're feeling at peace with the world.

The smoker who wants to give up should find it easier to do so if he or she is at the same time learning how to control his or her own response to stress.

51

Exercise regularly

Being physically fit won't automatically stop you ever suffering from stomach disorders but it will make you less likely to suffer from stomach problems or indeed from any other disorders. The person whose idea of exercise is getting up in the morning will be far more likely to suffer ill-effects when he or she is under pressure than the person who takes better care of his or her body.

If you are thinking of taking up exercise of any kind you should consult your doctor if you are taking any prescribed medicine, or if you are in any doubt about your fitness to undertake physical exercise.

Testing your fitness: Assuming that you don't have any real problems with your health, however, you'll first of all probably want to know just how fit you are. The tests which follow are designed to give you a rough idea of your physical condition. Should you develop any unusual pains or breathlessness while trying any of these tests you should obviously stop what you are doing straight away.

1   One of the simplest ways to find out how fit you are is to see how long you take to cover a mile. Anyone who is reasonably fit should be able to cover a mile within twelve minutes. It doesn't matter whether you walk, run, jog or mix all three.

2   A slightly more sophisticated test requires a step and a watch with a second hand. Most people can lay their hands on those two simple pieces of equipment. The step should be about 12 inches (0.3 metres) deep and the one at the bottom of the stairs is usually good enough. All you have to do for this test is step up and then step down again 24 times a minute, for three minutes. If your arithmetic is the same as mine that will mean that in the three-minute period you will have effectively climbed a total of 72 steps.

When you have completed the exercise, sit down and rest for 15 seconds. Then measure your heart rate during the subsequent 60 second period. If your pulse rate is below 80 a minute then you're really very fit. If your pulse rate is between 80 and 100 you're pretty fit. But if it is over 100 then you're really not looking after your body at all well.

Getting fit: Having come to some conclusion about your general state of health the next step is obviously to try and remedy any shortcomings. The first thing I want to point out here is that you really don't have to rush out and spend a fortune buying expensive exercise equipment. I find that there is something slightly ironic about the fact that our society is full of people who wouldn't dream of walking up stairs or crossing the road on foot, yet those same people enthusiastically spend money on rowing or cycling machines designed to give them much the same sort of exercise that they would have got if they had been less reliant on labour-saving gadgets in the first place!

Nor do I recommend that you rush out and join a sports club where the other members are enthusiastic competitors. There is now a lot of evidence to suggest that highly competitive sports are just as dangerous as any other type of stressful activity and it is certainly a fact that if you take up a sport in which you are expected to win medals, cups and competitions then although you may be getting the exercise you want you'll actually be adding to your stress load. It's a moot point in that case as to whether the increase in your general state of fitness balances out the increase in the total amount of stress to which you are exposed. However, there may be a public or private gymnasium near you where you can exercise in a comfortable and uncompetitive atmosphere.

Of all the other remaining types of exercise available there is none better than walking for improving your physical health without damaging your mental health. A gentle stroll round the town won't do your body much good but a fine brisk walk through the nearest park or over a few nearby fields will contribute enormously to your state of health.

The other advantage with walking, of course, is that you can actually relax your mind while you exercise. It's perfectly possible to get your daily daydream in at the same time as you take your regular constitutional. And walking for a mile or two away from the telephone and away from the pressures of modern-day living provides a tremendous opportunity for you to think out and resolve some of your problems.

Know where your stress comes from

In order to cope effectively with stress you must have some idea of what sort of things worry you the most. Study the check list which follows and answer 'yes' or 'no' to each of the questions. Every question to which you have answered 'yes' indicates a possible source of stress. Remember, however, that stress is by no means always bad for you and that life without stress is as tasteless and as unappealing as beef without mustard or eggs without salt. You need *some* stress in your life, but it's all a question of balance.

Do you wish you had more responsibility?

Do you feel that you have too much responsibility?

Do you hate your work?

Do you feel that you are under too much pressure at work?

Do you think that you are underpaid?

Do you think your workload is too great?

Do you feel that you are unappreciated at work?

Do you wish you obtained more satisfaction from your job?

Do you feel that your prospects for promotion are poor?

Do you worry about what will happen to you if you are promoted?

Do you think there are too many administrators where you work?

Do you worry about the danger associated with the work you do?

Do you dislike your working hours?

Do you find your workplace unpleasant?

Do you wish you had more pressure at work?

Do you find it difficult to talk to anyone at work?

Do you find the journey to work difficult or tiring?

Do you think that your race or sex has affected your chances of success at work?

Do you regularly skip lunch?

Do you get home late from work quite regularly?

Do you have to cancel holidays because of work?

Do you take work home with you?

Do you wish you had more friends?

Do you ever feel lonely?

Do you feel that getting married was a mistake?

Do you buy things you don't really need just to impress the neighbours?

Do you nightly have arguments about which television channel to watch?

Do you get annoyed by the noise your neighbours make?

Do you wish you had a room of your own in which you could get a little peace and quiet occasionally?

Do you find yourself always in a hurry?

Do you sometimes feel that your children simply use you as a convenient servant?

Do you find yourself having to be nice to people you dislike intensely?

Do you sometimes wish you could get on a plane and get away from it all?

Do you worry a lot about what other people think?

Do you talk to your spouse about things which really interest you?

Do you envy other people?

Do you always feel guilty if you do anything that you enjoy?

Do you feel that you are a burden to those around you?

Do you have to look after relatives who are a burden and a nuisance?

Do you feel bitter about the way you are treated at home?

Do you change your car if a new model comes out?

Do you have to telephone for a handyman if you buy a new appliance and it needs to have a plug fitted?

Do you live in a house that you cannot really afford?

Do you wish you had a hobby that you could really enjoy?

Do you worry a lot about your health?

Do you think you might have some serious disease?

Do you regularly buy medicines for yourself?

This list is by no means comprehensive but it is designed to give you some idea of the sort of things that are causing you stress. There are, of course, no simple slick answers to many of the problems listed here. If you find your work dull and boring you may not be able to do anything to change that now, but perhaps you could start some form of training programme that might enable you to get a better and more rewarding job at some later stage. Or perhaps, if finding another job really is very unlikely, you could take up some hobby or leisure interest which would provide you with the sense of personal satisfaction that your job does not give. One patient of mine who has a job he hates in a major car component factory breeds prize-winning budgerigars and has an international reputation for doing so. Another patient is a well-respected match fisherman, and although he finds his job as a local government clerk quite unsatisfying he gains a great deal of pleasure and pride from his hobby.

The important thing is that you should be aware of the things in your life which cause the greatest amount of stress. Only when you have satisfied the particular types of problem which cause you most stress will you be able to deal effectively with those stresses and strains.

Know yourself

In order to cope effectively with the stresses and strains which are today an integral part of life you must understand your own ambitions, fears and anxieties and you must learn a little about how you react to problems. Some self-awareness will make you far better equipped to cope with change and stress.

What are your priorities?:   Modern psychologists often use the word 'goals' to describe personal ambitions. It doesn't really matter what terminology you use, but it does matter that you understand your own priorities. What comes first in your life? Your job? Your home? Your family? Your hobby? Your friends? Is money more important than sex and is power more important than money to you? Only by understanding your own priorities will you be able to make vital decisions quickly and wisely. If, for example, your boss tells you that you've got to attend a business meeting on the day that your daughter is in a school play for the very first time you'll have to make an important decision. You won't be able to make that decision unless you know precisely where your priorities lie.

What are your faults?   It's often said that the things we complain about in other people are the things we ourselves are guilty of. So, for example, if you're always very upset by people who are inattentive when you're telling a story or anecdote then perhaps you ought to consider whether you are always as attentive as you could be when others are telling you their favourite stories.

Are you more critical of yourself than you would be of others?   A patient of mine once worried herself into the operating theatre by imagining that her friends would all consider her heartless for having refused to have her elderly but vituperative mother-in-

57

law to live with her. After she'd had her operation to deal with a peptic ulcer I asked her whether she would have been dismayed if any of her friends had refused to have their mothers-in-law to live with them. She admitted that she would have supported their decisions wholeheartedly. I pointed out that her friends almost certainly felt the same way towards her.

What habits have you got?   Habits can be useful. For example, it's useful to get into the habit of cleaning your teeth regularly without having to remember to go and do it. But habits can also be annoying, harmful and a sign of excessive exposure to stress.

They can be annoying — because if you keep humming short snatches from the same tune you're likely to drive those around you quite insane.

They can be harmful — because if you stop at the pub every evening on the way home from work you're quite likely to develop a habit that you can't easily break.

And they can be a sign of tension too. Floor-pacing, pencil tapping, nail-chewing, ear-scratching, knuckle-cracking — all these are warning signs that there is a little bit too much stress around. If you can learn to be aware of these habits you can use them as a guide to the level of your stress exposure.

Do you blame others for your own shortcomings?   The workman who isn't very good will usually blame his tools. The housewife whose cooking skills are limited will often blame her oven. The golfer who spends most of his time looking for his ball will blame his clubs. The gardener whose seeds don't grow will blame the quality of his soil. We all do it; and when we're putting our blame onto some inanimate objects it's probably a harmless enough way to get rid of our own feelings of inadequacy.

But when we put the blame for things we ourselves should or should not have done onto other people then things become rather more complicated. The shop manager who blames the counter-assistant for not telling him that he hadn't ordered any more supplies is probably being unfair. The man who blames his

58

wife for not looking after the family finances more effectively may well feel inadequate for having failed to earn more money, or guilty for having spent so much on beer and cigarettes.

Blaming others unnecessarily can produce problems in a number of ways. The person who has been blamed may well feel resentful and that can contribute to a deterioration in your relationship with that individual. It won't matter too much if the individual concerned is one with whom you do not have a close relationship, but if he or she is someone close to you then this resentment can cause quite significant problems.

And even when the individual you've blamed isn't someone that you know well you may suffer from tremendous feelings of guilt afterwards.

Do you always yearn for yesterday? Our society is an ever-changing one and many people find it extremely difficult to accept that things will never be what they once were. But yearning for the good old days doesn't help anyone. If you spend your time wishing that life was as it used to be, then you're quite likely to become bitter and twisted and probably annoy those around you. Enjoy your memories but don't let them interfere with the present.

If you spend a little time learning just how you respond to stress then you will be far better able to limit the damage that stress can do to you, and you will be in a far stronger position to improve your capacity for dealing with stress.

Learn to relax

Many of the patients I have met over the years have been slightly worried when I have suggested that they learn to relax. Some have immediately insisted that they could never do 'anything like that'. Others have looked at me with some concern, obviously suspecting that something must have got to me and turned me away from orthodox medicine and towards the 'fringe' world.

I can understand this reaction because in recent years relaxation has been associated very often with areas of health care which owe more to the world of show business than science. It has been very fashionable for some entertainers to talk about relaxation in a mystical, semi-religious way and I feel very strongly that this unhappy association must have worried many people who might otherwise have contemplated relaxation therapy with equanimity.

The great tragedy in all this is that a very effective form of therapy has been partly lost to many thousands of people because of its bizarre associations. The truth is that the various different forms of relaxation therapy which are available are known to work very well, and can often contribute a great deal to the health of those who are prepared to spend just a little time and effort learning how best to take advantage of these techniques. Research workers in institutions with solid scientific reputations have repeatedly shown the value of different forms of relaxation therapy, and their results have now been published in most of the world's leading medical and scientific journals.

For those who want to learn how to relax with the help of professional advisers there are many institutions and courses available. Hypnosis, biofeedback, yoga and transcendental meditation are just four of the techniques which are used quite regularly by many professionals in order to help patients learn how to relax.

However, I don't believe that it is necessary to join any organization, go anywhere or pay any money in order to learn how best to relax your body and your mind. I believe that you can learn how to relax perfectly well at home. And by relaxing you can learn how to cope with stress more effectively and how to build up your resistance to stress.

Before beginning to describe how best you can learn how to relax I just want to point out that you must be prepared to practise a little to start with. No one would expect to be able to play a game of tennis or dance the tango without a little practice and exactly the same thing is true of relaxation. And just as you will get better at golf or dancing the more you try it so you will get better at relaxing if you continue to practise regularly.

Relaxing your mind

There are many ways in which you can learn to relax your mind and banish the problems and worries that cause so much damage. But I believe that one of the very best ways to relax your mind is to learn how to daydream properly. Some of the purists who teach meditation professionally claim that to relax your mind properly you should aim at removing all thoughts from your conscious brain and attempt to replace those thoughts with a void. In other words, they believe that to relax your mind fully you shouldn't be thinking of anything at all.

Now although I recognize that this type of mental relaxation is extremely effective, I don't honestly believe that it is necessary to get rid of all mental processes in order to relax, and I rather suspect that most people will find it very difficult to get rid of all their thoughts. If you try it you'll see what I mean; you push out your worries about the holidays or about the car and they're just replaced by worries about the washing machine and the lawn-mower. Most of us find it extremely difficult not to think about *anything*.

It is, however, relatively easy to learn how to replace un-pleasant, stressful thoughts with pleasant, relaxing thoughts and if you learn to do this then you will be protecting yourself from the effects of those stressful thoughts just as effectively as if you'd managed to empty your mind completely.

Daydreaming: Daydreaming is one of those valuable talents which most of us lose when we grow up. As children we're pretty good at it but as we grow older it's a trick we lose. People complain when we daydream and eventually we begin to feel guilty if we sit or stand thinking about pleasant memories and not getting on with whatever it is we're supposed to be doing.

So it's something that most people have to relearn. To begin with it is something that is probably easier to do in a calm quiet spot rather than somewhere busy where people are milling around and there are all sorts of distractions. I don't believe that there is anyone so busy that they can't grab a minute or two once or twice a day in order to practise a little daydreaming. The beauty of this simple technique is, of course, that you can practise it just about anywhere. A lot of people find the bathroom a perfect spot because they don't have to find any excuse for being alone for a few minutes.

It doesn't really matter what you think of when you are daydreaming as long as it's a pleasant memory and one that doesn't get you too excited. I must stress that there really is a difference between daydreaming and fantasizing, for example, and that although a good strong sexual fantasy is very healthy it isn't really the right sort of way to get rid of your tensions. If you spend your daydreaming time thinking about your favourite sex object you'll probably do your stomach more harm than good because powerful sex fantasies are stressful rather than relaxing. For relaxation purposes you're much better off thinking about a peaceful day in the country, a gentle day on the beach or a good evening out at a quiet restaurant.

You can actually prove to yourself that your body is relaxing when you are daydreaming by measuring your pulse. Before you start relaxing feel and count your pulse for a full minute. Use the forefinger of your left hand and press it lightly against the radial artery which can be found in the area at the base of your right thumb. If you measure your pulse rate again when you've exchanged your worries about having just smashed the car for the third time in a week for a happy memory of a day spent soaking up the sun you'll find that your pulse rate will have fallen.

With a little practice, of course, you should be able to daydream so effectively that you can hear the breeze rustling though the trees and feel the heat of the sun on your skin. With more practice you'll be able to daydream very successfully in circumstances where there are all sorts of other distractions. You should, for example, be able to daydream very comfortably in a busy store, in a traffic queue or on a crowded train.

Relaxing your body

In order to relax your body properly you must first learn just how your muscles feel when they are tense and tight. To begin with, therefore, try clenching your fist as hard as you can. If you look at your hand and keep trying to push your fingertips into the palm of your hand you'll see the skin changing colour and feel the muscles becoming harder and harder. Once you've done that you must immediately try to relax those same muscles. Unfold your first and let your hand go as loose and as floppy as you can. The contrast is important because it is only by clenching your muscles that you can really expect to know what your muscles feel like when they are relaxed.

Relaxing your muscles: 12 steps: You can of course try clenching and relaxing the muscles of your hand almost anywhere, but to learn how to relax all your muscles you probably need to start somewhere quiet and private where you aren't going to be suddenly disturbed. If you feel at all embarrassed about what you are doing then lock the door so that you won't suddenly be surprised by someone coming in unexpectedly. It will take a full fifteen minutes to relax all the muscles of your body and you'll find it easier to begin with if you relax lying down on a bed or sofa. If you haven't got a bed or sofa in the room you've chosen lie on the floor, but use pillows or cushions to make sure that you're comfortable before you start, or you'll never manage to relax successfully.

1   Begin again by clenching the muscles of your left hand and making as tight a fist as you can. Once you've done that let your fist unfold quite suddenly. The muscles of your left hand should now be limp and relaxed.

2   Next bend your left arm so that your biceps muscle stands out as much as you can make it. Use one of those poses that bodybuilders favour. And as soon as you've managed to get the muscle really taut and tight reverse the process and let your biceps

muscle relax. Let the whole arm just lie or hang limply by your side.

3 Your right hand is the next one to tackle and this should be followed by your right biceps muscle. If you're lying flat on your back when you do this you should now have two very limp, flaccid arms lying useless by your sides. Incidentally, if you find it difficult to remember these instructions you can either get someone to read them out to you, or record them onto a tape-player and then relax as the instructions are given. Allow a good 30 second gap between each set of instructions.

4 Having relaxed the muscles of your hands and arms you should now move on to the muscles of your feet and legs. Begin this part of the exercise by curling the toes of your left foot and tightening the muscles of the foot as well. As soon as the foot and toes feel as tight and as tense as you can make them relax the foot and the toes completely.

5 Once you've relaxed your left foot move onto your left calf muscle. Tense the muscles at the back of your leg so that if you reach down with your hand you can feel the muscles there tight and hard. Bend your foot at the ankle to help tighten up the muscles even more.

6 When you've managed to get your calf muscles really tight relax them, and then try to push your foot as far away from you as you can. This exercise will tighten up the muscles on the front of your thigh. Relax these and then repeat all these foot and leg exercises on the right side.

7 The next step is to tighten up your buttock muscles as much as you can. If you do this properly you should be able to lift your whole body upwards off the bed an inch or two. Then, when you've tightened and relaxed these muscles move on to your abdominal muscles. Try to pull your navel as far into your body as it will go and then try to relax it so that your waist circumference reaches its horrendous worst.

8 The chest muscles come next and these are fairly easy to tighten. All you need to do is take in a very big breath and hold it for as long as possible. Then, when you feel as though you're about to burst, let the air out and allow your chest muscles to relax.

9 To tighten up the muscles of your shoulders push your shoulders backwards as far as they will go and then turn them inwards and forwards in an attempt to touch your face with your shoulder bones. You should not be able to do this. Follow this by shrugging your shoulders upwards so that your head disappears into your neck. Then when you've tried all these extraordinary exercises try and let your shoulder muscles relax.

10 Follow this by tightening up the muscles of your back by trying to make yourself as tall as you can and then, when you're relaxed those muscles, by working on your neck muscles. Lift your head forwards and pull on the muscles at the back of your neck; turn your head first one way and then the other as far as it will go and push your head backwards with as much force as you can muster. Then let all these muscles relax and move your head about so that you can make sure that it is really completely loose and easy.

11 The muscles of your face are fairly easy to tense. Move your eyebrows upwards and then pull them down as far as they will go. Screw your eyes up as tightly as you can and try to keep them shut. Grit your teeth, wrinkle your nose, move your jaw around, smile as wide as you can and grimace at some imaginary enemy. Push your tongue out and wriggle it around all over the place. And don't forget to relax each of these muscles as soon as you've tightened it effectively.

By now if you've been doing this whole exercise properly you should be feeling very limp and relaxed. Your breathing should be slow and regular and you should feel quite sleepy.

The whole procedure shouldn't have taken more than fifteen or twenty minutes, and when you've practised a little more on your bed you should be quite capable of conducting most of these simple exercises in just about any environment.

Learn to escape

Hard work: A patient of mine who had persistent indigestion once came to see me to ask how best he could deal with his problem. I knew that the main cause of his distress was the fact that he and his wife ran a small corner newspaper shop. They worked every day from about five-thirty a.m. to about eight in the evening. They worked on Saturdays and Sundays and on bank holidays as well. They hadn't had a holiday for years.

Knowing that this hard-working schedule was contributing a great deal to the indigestion I suggested that it might be a good idea if he and his wife took a few days away. I pointed out to him that the money he was making wasn't going to be much good if he wasn't around to enjoy spending it. Rather to my surprise my patient agreed to the suggestion. He came into the surgery four days later to ask me to sign his passport application form.

I didn't see him again for two months and then he came into the surgery looking very glum. I asked him what was the matter.

'I thought you said I'd feel better after a break,' he complained.

'Don't you?'

'I feel worse,' he moaned. 'I was glad to get back to the shop.'

'Where on earth did you go?' I asked him. 'What sort of holiday did you take?'

To my utter amazement my patient told me that he and his wife had decided that since they hadn't had a holiday for such a long time they would try to cram as much as they could into the fortnight they'd finally managed to grab away from their store. So they'd booked the car onto a cross-channel ferry, filled it with provisions and set off to drive around as much of Europe as they could cover in fourteen days. They'd eventually managed to criss-cross through France, Germany, Luxembourg, Holland,

Austria, Belgium, Switzerland and Italy. They'd slept occasionally in small hotels and once or twice in their car. They'd covered an average of just over 480 kilometres (300 miles) a day and they'd arrived home totally exhausted.

My patient honestly didn't seem to understand that what he and his wife really needed was a good old-fashioned holiday where they could wander around aimlessly for hours at a time, where they could lie in bed a little later, where they could spoil themselves, enjoy themselves, get to know one another again and generally relax.

More worries: Not that my shopkeeper patient is by any means unique. I have another patient who works as a factory manager and he had a proven peptic ulcer about two years ago. He took cimetidine for a month or two but eventually needed an operation. After the operation he swore that he would relax a little more and take life a little more gently.

To help him do just that he bought a small cottage in the country where he assured me he would be able to get away from all his problems. And he was quite right in that he certainly did get away from his problems at work. But all he did was exchange his worries about the factory for worries about his cottage. The drainpipes got blocked regularly with leaves from the trees. The roof leaked on two occasions. Part of the chimneystack fell in. There was dry rot in the kitchen. The problems just went on and on and my factory manager patient found himself worrying just as much about his cottage as he was worrying about his job. He acquired a second peptic ulcer.

Both these patients had the right basic idea but both failed to realize that there is very little point in exchanging one set of stresses for another set of stresses. What they needed was not another bunch of problems to worry about but a few days complete break every now and again.

Both the factory manager and the shopkeeper would have benefited much more if they'd chosen to spend their holidays in small hotels or boarding houses where they could have allowed themselves to relax properly and where they could have forgotten their worries and problems completely.

Indeed, they would probably have had a much more beneficial break if they had stayed at home, switched off their telephone, locked their front doors and settled down in front of the TV with a pile of good books and magazines to read.

Incidentally, before leaving the subject of 'escape' I must mention the fact that many very busy people have learned to escape from their day-to-day worries for a few minutes at a time by using children's games. Executive toys are something of a joke to some people but they do help a great deal by enabling the executive to regress to his childhood in a moment of crisis. The fact that the toys are well made and expensive means that he can do this without losing any status. I firmly believe that children's toys such as puzzles and other games are an excellent way to switch off from problems that are causing tremendous stress. And by offering a minor challenge on a completely different level they allow the individual concerned to regain his strength and to return to the original, main problem with renewed vigour and recharged batteries.

My study is littered with games and puzzles of all kinds!

Let your emotions hang out

Forty years ago George Young had a small market stall on which he sold all sorts of miscellaneous items. I don't think there was anything he wouldn't have sold if he thought he could have found a buyer with a little enthusiasm and some cash. Through hard work and a considerable amount of business acumen he built up his business from that single market stall until it consisted of a chain of retail shops selling groceries.

He was justifiably proud of that chain of stores and it was, I know, with some regret that he eventually accepted a bid from a huge international company which wanted to add his chain to their own collection of stores. I don't think he would have accepted the offer at all if he had any children but since he had no heir he was, I think, well aware that the shops had to be managed by someone else eventually.

While negotiating the sale of his shops George had successfully managed to persuade the directors of the major company to allow him to continue to run his own business. He wanted to run things in much the same sort of way that he had always done and the international company was apparently keen enough to buy his stores to agree to his request.

When the takeover finally took place, therefore, George was really not too upset. He still imagined that he would have very much the same sort of control over the day-to-day running of his shops as he had had before and he still thought of them as 'his' shops.

But, of course, that's not the way that big business is run; within two days of the takeover being completed the big international company had sent round a team of men to take down the signs over George's shops and replace them with their own signs. The day after that they sent round a personnel officer to vet all the staff and the day after that they began to organize an army of shopfitters whose task it was to strip all the shops to the walls and refurnish them entirely.

George was horrified and when he heard what was going on he immediately telephoned the chairman of the international company that had bought his shops to protest. That was when he discovered how different things really were going to be now that the trading courtship was over. The chairman, who prior to the takeover had happily taken all his calls, laughed at all his jokes and been enthusiastic about every one of George's pet projects was suddenly unavailable. George found himself talking to an assistant; a young man with a haughty manner, a condescending voice and a total disregard for Geroge's own ambitions, hopes and aspirations.

That was just the beginning. Things slowly got worse during the days and weeks that followed. George found that although he had expected to be allowed to have some day-to-day control over his shops he was, in practice, given virtually no control at all. Buying was all done from a central department. Advertising was organized by an agency. Staff recruitment was managed by the personnel officer. And George found himself sitting in his own expensively furnished office playing with the paperclips.

To begin with he managed to disguise from his colleagues and friends the extent of his disappointment. At the golf club he remained his usual quietly humorous self. At home he managed to exhibit tremendous self-control. There were no signs anywhere of his sadness and sorrow and none of those close to him had any idea that George was suffering.

He came to me for help because although he thought he was managing to cope well with his problems George suddenly found himself experiencing extraordinary feelings of violence. He had never hit anyone in anger in his life and yet suddenly he found himself worrying that he might suddenly kill someone. The fears were so real that he found himself in a cold sweat every time he passed the toolbench in the garage or saw a knife in the kitchen. And what made these strange feelings so remarkable and so terrifying as far as George was concerned was the fact that the person he felt that he wanted to kill was his wife.

'Why do I want to kill her?' George wanted to know. 'Why don't I want to kill the chairman of that damned company. Or his wretched young assistant?'

I explained to him that what was happening was that he was displacing the anger and frustration that he felt and that it was because he had made such an effort to disguise his feelings towards his new employer that George found himself unable even to enjoy the idea of destroying him in a fantasy. George's determination to disguise his personal feelings had left him twisted and distorted inside and he was subconsciously attempting to redirect some of that anger. His wife just happend to be the closest person to him and therefore the most likely target for his displaced aggression.

I've related that story because I think it illustrates very well why we should always endeavour to let our feelings out rather than bottle them up inside us. I'm not suggesting that George really would have taken a knife to his wife, but I do believe that there was a real risk of him suffering considerably more anguish as a result of the feelings he would not allow himself to express. When I saw him he was beginning to feel guilty because of his apparently inexplicable feelings towards his wife. Before long he would have probably begun to resent the fact that she was unwittingly making him feel guilty. And so it would go on.

It could have all been avoided if only George had allowed himself to get rid of his feelings of anger and annoyance rather more naturally. If he'd screamed and shouted at someone, or if he'd thrown a tantrum, he would have lost a little dignity but he would have felt very much better afterwards. And, most important of all, he would have got some of the aggression out of his system.

But for many people like George, of course, it isn't that easy to allow emotional feelings to show. After all we are often taught as children that we should always try to hide our emotions. We are taught that it is wrong to allow others to see us getting angry. Children, and boys in particular, are taught that it is wrong to cry in public. And there seems to be a very well-established tradition that it is much better to bottle up fears, anxieties and anger and suffer in silence rather than to let ourselves go and let others see just how we feel.

I firmly believe that bottling up emotions like this produces two types of damage. To begin with I think that it is partly because of the fact that we all try to hide our emotions from one another that there is so much violence in our society. One particular type of violence that often occurs more or less directly as a result of emotions being bottled up is baby battering. The young mother who is alone and worried and not really capable of coping with her child will often store up so much anger against the world in general that eventually she just takes it all out on her baby.

And I also believe that bottled up emotions can cause internal damage too, producing all the standard stress-induced diseases such as headaches, asthma and peptic ulcers. If you are an ulcer victim or an indigestion sufferer and you have a tendency to bottle up your feelings and refrain from letting other people know how you feel then I think that there is a very good chance that the two things are related. Your stored emotional feelings are very probably responsible for your stomach symptoms.

Relieving yourself of emotions: There are two important ways in which you can relieve yourself of your stored emotions without actually telling the people around you exactly what you think about them and without actually getting up in the middle of the next Parent-Teachers Association meeting and smashing the headmaster over the head with a ruler.

The first thing you should do is to learn to cry when you are sad. Tears are an important safety valve and an acknowledgment that you have reached crisis point. They provide instant relief from frustration and are a sign that you have accepted your own distress.

Boys are sometimes taught that it is always unmanly to cry. This is nonsense. Tears can be a sign of strength not weakness. And after the tears there should come a time of calm and peaceful sleep. Tears can be an essential part of the stress control programme.

The second way in which you can get rid of those bottled up emotions is by learning to express your feelings of aggression in a relatively harmless way. And there are lots of ways in which you can do just that.

I recently read with great joy of a fairly senior official attending an International Monetary Fund meeting who was so exasperated by his colleagues that he walked out of the meeting, crossed the road, went into a funfair and proceeded to throw wooden balls at china plates until he'd got rid of all his tension. I thought that was a truly marvellous way to deal with an impending crisis, for smashing china is a really pleasing way of relieving tension and getting rid of aggressive feelings. The Greeks do it particularly well and they love smashing plates during a good evening out in a restaurant.

72

But there are plenty of other techniques you can try. Swing-balls and punchbags are ideal objects to hit. You can't damage them and they won't hit back. At home you could try beating the carpet or knocking the stuffing out of the mattress. At the office you could perhaps club together with a few colleagues to pay for an effigy of someone you all love to hate.

Showing aggression in this sort of way is sometimes said to be immature. I don't think it is. On the contrary, I think it is a sign of maturity and wisdom to be able to release your accumulated tensions in such a deliberate and sensible way.

Respect the four cornerstones

Any builder will tell you that if you are making structural alterations to a house you won't, if you've got any sense, mess about with all four corners of the building at once. You'll probably be able to get away with making changes at one corner at a time, but if you try doing anything as foolish as leaving the house standing on just one cornerstone then you'll probably destroy the whole building.

Human life is a bit like that in so far as most of us need to have some stable parts in our world if we are to survive. And the four cornerstones in most lives are family, work, friends and leisure. Problems really arise when for any reason all those four areas are affected at once.

Kenny Orville: One patient of mine exhibited only too well the sort of problems which can arise when the four cornerstones are all disturbed at once. Kenny Orville had been married for seven years when I first saw him and had worked for a year longer than that in the same office of a large travel agency.

His marriage had slowly been crumbling for nearly half its length, and it finally fell apart as a result of a row about whether or not the Orvilles should have their annual summer holiday in France or Germany. It had been an unhappy marriage for some time and I don't think either partner was entirely sad to see the

73

relationship finally and formally broken.

In some ways Kenny was actually relieved that he no longer had to go on pretending to love the woman with whom he lived and I suspect that the breakup of his marriage would, had it been the only major event in his life at that time, have been of remarkably little consequence to him.

However, two days after his marriage had finally fallen apart Kenny fulfilled the ambition of his working life and told his employer exactly what he thought of him. He also told him precisely what he could do with his job. This quite naturally meant that Kenny was now not only separated but also unemployed, and since most of his friends worked at the travel agency it also meant that he was separated from them as well.

When he came to see me a week after all this had happened Kenny Orville was suffering from quite acute pains in his upper abdomen. He was feeling nauseated most of the time, his appetite had more or less disappeared and he was swallowing biscuits by the handful and glasses of milk by the dozen in a vain attempt to keep the pain in his stomach under control. When I talked to him he admitted that he had suffered from various pains in his upper abdomen for the best part of nine months but he insisted that none of the pains had been anywhere near as bad as the one that he had developed in the last few days.

To begin with I gave him a prescription for an antacid mixture and a mild tranquillizer. I felt he needed these for a day or two in order to help cut into the acute anxiety state into which he had sunk.

I had also planned to get a barium meal examination of his stomach done at the local hospital, but things moved faster than I'd anticipated and that same night I got a telephone call from Kenny to tell me that the pain in his stomach was rapidly becoming quite unbearable. He was living in a small boarding house and when I got there he was writhing around in obviously severe pain.

It turned out that Kenny's peptic ulcer had perforated and he needed an operation in order to repair the damage that had been done. Now it is, of course, quite impossible to prove that Kenny's sudden deterioration was directly connected to his loss of two of his life's cornerstones, but in my view it was no coincidence that his stomach problem deteriorated when it did. Kenny had made the almost fatal mistake of making dramatic changes in two important parts of his life at the same time. The resultant stress had been too much for his stomach to bear and Kenny had suffered accordingly.

Peter Roberts: Peter Roberts was another patient of mine whose stomach problems became much worse when he made dramatic changes in his lifestyle. Peter worked as a sales representative for a food manufacturer and he was, I understand, extremely good at his job. He was certainly good enough to impress his superiors in the firm for they promoted him to a job as sales manager in another part of the country. Now, although it may be rather difficult for people who are unemployed to accept, getting promoted can be an extremely stressful business. And Peter Roberts tackled his promotion in a way almost designed to ensure that all his family felt the stresses as acutely as possible.

Two days after he had been informed of his promotion Peter took his wife and their two nine-year-old twin daughters down to the area where he was going to be sales manager and started house hunting. The company for which he worked was a large international concern which didn't like its employees to hang around, so Peter had something like two weeks in which to prepare and plan his move.

Now as anyone who has ever moved house will confirm there are a good many problems to be overcome. There are the legal and contractual problems associated with selling one home and buying another. There are the problem of buying carpets and curtains, arranging for furniture removers to call, informing the telephone company, the gas people and the electricity suppliers, and, of course, finding a new school. To try and manage all this in one two-week period is expecting a good deal of everyone concerned. To try and manage it all in one two-week period while you're tying up the loose ends from one job and preparing to start unravelling the loose ends from another job, as Peter Roberts was, is asking for trouble.

And Peter Roberts found his trouble. He ended up spending the day he should have been moving house in one of our local hospitals being investigated for chest pains. It was thought at first that the pains were due to heart trouble. It was only later that it became clear that what he had really been suffering from was severe indigestion caused by stress.

He would perhaps have been wiser to have moved into a hotel in the area where he was going to work and to have settled into his new job first before trying to move house and home. The stress of commuting and being away from his family during the week would almost certainly have been less than the stress of trying to cope with a major upheaval involving four cornerstones at once.

Be prepared to say 'no'

June Harper was a foreman in a local car component factory and she hated her job. She had accepted the post only because no one else really wanted it and she had not had the temerity to refuse when the firm's works manager had offered it to her. She found the job distasteful because she was now isolated from her former friends yet still not part of the management hierarchy. She felt that she was in a limbo in between the shop floor and the top level management group.

In addition to her position as a works foreman Mrs Harper was also a member of an enormous range of committees. She was secretary of her local Womens Institute Group, treasurer of the Parent-Teachers Association, and on half-a-dozen other assorted committees. Whenever there was a local flagday to organize on behalf of some charity or other she would find herself standing around with a can and a tray of flowers. Most of her weekday evenings were spent sitting in either draughty church halls listening to boring speeches or in a spare bedroom at home going through sheaves of paperwork. She didn't like the committee work or the paperwork, and she found herself getting more and more stressed by the fact that so many people seemed determined to impose on her goodwill.

I asked her why she had allowed herself to get involved in so many activities that she didn't enjoy and she confessed that the reason was really quite simple. She just couldn't say 'no'.

'I always feel so guilty,' she confessed. 'People ask me to do things and although I don't really want to do them at all I say "yes" because I don't want to be rude or offensive'.

There are lots of people like Mrs Harper, and unfortunately there are also lots of people who are prepared to take advantage of those who find it too difficult to say 'no'.

In general, I think that it is fair to say that the people who suffer most from this inability to avoid getting committed to projects in which they themselves have no real interest are those individuals who are overimbued with such good qualities as generosity, kindness and compassion.

There is no simple answer to this particular type of problem, of course, for if you are the sort of person who finds it difficult to say 'no' then you really aren't ever going to find it easy to turn down requests for help.

Still, you should try. And you might find it easier if you remember that the people who keep asking for your help are simply taking advantage of your generous nature.

Plan ahead!

Few things are more stressful than the things we don't expect. Sudden crises, disasters of any kind and unforeseen accidents can all cause a great deal of stress or illness. And yet many of the problems which do cause us great distress and which seem to be unforeseeable are in fact preventable. If only we would learn to plan ahead a little more then we would all be able to minimize our exposure to stress.

Being organized minimizes stress: I remember when I worked

77

in a casualty department at one busy general hospital being amazed at just how rarely were there any real crises. There were many very ill patients being brought into the department and many potential crises. But things were organized so well and planned so carefully that in practice most of those potential crises could be treated as fairly routine problems.

I spent some time one day watching how the casualty sister in charge of the department made sure that everything was always well organized. Whenever the department was quiet, for example, she would send two nurses around every cupboard and every cubicle to check that the supplies of syringes, needles and drugs were kept fully stocked. She regularly tested all the electrical equipment to make sure that everything was working. And pieces of equipment that were really vital were duplicated. There were, for example, two defibrillators in the resuscitation room.

At another hospital where I once worked things were very different. There the sister in charge was really quite disorganized, and whenever an emergency was brought into the department there was quite a panic as people rushed about looking for the bits and pieces of equipment that they needed.

Someone would discover that the stethoscope had been borrowed. And then it would turn out that the electrocardiograph machine wasn't working because the plug had been taken off and put onto the fridge. There wouldn't be a syringe of the right size available, and a nurse would have to be despatched at top speed to another part of the hospital.

The result was that when there was an emergency everyone *knew* that was an emergency. And, not only was the unfortunate patient not treated anywhere near as well as a patient in a well-organized department but the staff found themselves suffering from a great deal of unnecessary stress as well.

We can all benefit from the example set by that well-organized casualty sister and we can all organize our lives much better than we do. Writing things down in a notebook is a good start since few of us have perfect memories. Most of us benefit if we have a written list to jog our memories from time to time.

It's also a good idea to keep letters, bills, receipts and so on properly filed. Struggling to find the right piece of paper may not sound too much of a problem but if you have to do it once a month it can add that little bit of extra stress to your life. If you don't want to buy a filing cabinet then put your papers into large, old brown envelopes and simply write a description of the contents on the outside of each envelope.

When you're planning some special event keep a master plan and a special diary in which you mark off details of the dates by which time all the various problems need to have been solved. That way you won't suddenly find that you've organized a wonderful party but forgotten to send out the invitations.

Coping with domestic problems: It is also a good idea to learn to cope with minor problems in and around the home. It is becoming increasingly difficult to get hold of doctors, handymen and repairmen of all kinds. The individual who can deal with minor illnesses and minor incidences of material fragility himself without having to rely on the goodwill of an outsider will be far less likely to suffer stress waiting for a little action.

And finally it is also worth while preparing for the almost inevitable breakdown of the electricity or gas supply at some time in the next twelve months. Buy a spare lamp or some candles and try to obtain some form of alternative heating and cooking.

If you can avoid these possibly minor and probably temporary inconveniences by planning ahead then you will be helping to limit your own exposure to stress.

Be prepared to complain

Don't be afraid to complain and do learn to regard bureaucratic institutions of all kinds with a healthy measure of disrespect.

There are few things more likely to produce stress than buying some much-wanted item, getting it home, taking it out of its box and finding out that it doesn't work. If that happens to you and the shop owner tells you that it isn't his problem now that you've bought it, let him know that you're not going to be fobbed off with any miserable excuse but that you're going to take your complaint right to the top.

That might make him change his mind but if it doesn't then do make sure that you complain. Write letters to the company which made the product and make sure that you get in touch with all the consumer protection agencies that could possibly be interested in your plight.

That way you may get a replacement, the company may try harder to ensure that the next customer is better satisfied and you'll probably be far less annoyed about the whole thing. If you're worried that you'll say something you might regret write a letter of complaint, keep it for 24 hours and see if you still feel the same about it then. Waiting 24 hours protects you against your own impetuosity, but at least you'll have been able to get some of your anger out of your system.

Take the same attitude towards officials of all kinds. They're employed to help make your life easier not harder. And if they don't seem to understand that, find someone who does.

5

Ten-point Survival Plan

If you try following the suggestions listed below you will find that a great deal of the stress in your life can be eliminated.

1. *If you have persistent or recurrent pains which you think are in or around your stomach then you should see your doctor.*   Similarly you should seek medical advice if you have any other symptoms which may signify a lesion affecting the upper part of your gastrointestinal tract. Your doctor will often be able to make a firm diagnosis in the surgery, but if he is uncertain as to the precise nature of your illness he will be able to organize the necessary investigations. The great majority of stomach X-rays and endoscopy examinations show no signs of any active lesions, but they do at least provide some comfort by eliminating the possibility of there being any serious disorder. The main point in going to see your doctor if you have problems with your stomach is to get a firm diagnosis.

2. *Once he has made a diagnosis your doctor will usually offer some form of therapy.*   Unfortunately the type of treatment that doctors offer is usually designed only to deal with the symptoms rather than to affect the cause of the problem. Your doctor may be able to help clear up your stomach trouble, but there is a good chance that exactly the same symptoms will recur unless you are able to do something to help yourself.

3. *Try to limit your exposure to stress.*   From what is known about the development of stomach ulcers, indigestion and other gastric problems it is reasonable to assert that the best way to protect yourself from future stomach disorders is to limit your exposure to stress or to improve your capacity to cope with stress. Stress is known to cause and exacerbate many stomach lesions. By limiting your exposure to stress or by 'stress-proofing' your

body you will be able to provide yourself with some permanent protection against a stress-induced stomach problem.

4. *In order to protect yourself against the ravages of stress you must first learn something about the pressures in your life.*　You must understand precisely what sort of problems are likely to give you the greatest amount of distress and you must try to understand the sort of circumstances in which you are most likely to find yourself exposed to damaging stress. Once you have succeeded in identifying the most damaging stresses in your life then you must attempt to limit your involvement in outside affairs so that the damage done to your body is kept to a minimum. It is also important that you do not allow other people to put you under pressure by making excessive demands on you. Finally, you should also make sure that if you are planning any change in one of the four cornerstones of your life — family, work, friends and leisure — the other cornerstones are allowed to remain relatively undisturbed. If you make changes in all these areas at the same time then you will be putting yourself under an extraordinary amount of stress.

5. *Try to plan your life.*　Unexpected events and unforeseen pressures do the most amount of damage. If you can organize the way you live so that you are exposed to a limited number of sudden crises then you will be helping to protect yourself against stress.

6. *In order to improve your capacity to withstand stress it is important that you do all that you can to become physically fit.*　The two most important things to remember are that you should eat carefully and wisely and that you should take a moderate amount of regular exercise.

Irregular eating habits will not only damage your stomach directly by allowing acid to harm the delicate wall of your stomach but they will also damage your good health. And good physical health is an important asset in the fight against stress.

It is important to remember that giving up or reducing your intake of cigarettes and alcohol will have a dramatic and positive effect on the physical state of your stomach lining. Both cigarettes and alcohol irritate and inflame the stomach lining and make it more than usually susceptible to stomach acid. The more you learn to control your stress the less you will need the help of such artificial aids as tobacco and alcohol.

7. *Improve your mental capacity to cope with stress by letting your emotions show*.   Don't try to bottle up everything, for if you do you will eventually find yourself unable to cope with even fairly minor problems. However capable we may think ourselves to be each one of us has a trigger point, and the wisest way to avoid encountering any problems as a result of exposure to stress is to try and ensure that your daily level of exposure to stress is kept within your own personal limit. If you bottle up your emotions and refuse to let those around you see when you are sad or angry then you will be storing up your stresses and reducing your natural capacity to deal with the unexpected.

8. *Learn how to relax your body*.   Physical relaxation programmes have a rather unfortunate reputation at the moment; and I suspect that this is largely the fault of those religious groups who seem to argue that in order to practise relaxation it is necessary to shave off all head hair, to wear yellow-coloured robes and to wander up and down the streets of the biggest main city in the neighbourhood in an attempt to sell copies of long-playing records.

In practice, nothing could be further from the truth. In order to relax properly you do not have to spend any money, join any specific organization or buy any equipment. All you need to do is to follow the simple physical relaxation plan outlined in chapter 4 (page 63) and then use the technique should you ever feel early signs of pressure building up or stress developing.

9. *Learn how to relax your mind*.   Once you have mastered the

art of physically relaxing your body you should learn how to relax mentally. Many people say that they just cannot relax. I agree that some of the self-hypnosis programmes advocated by the most enthusiastic experts sound daunting to the uninitiated. In practice, however, you do not have to attempt anything so complex in order to achieve a useful level of mental relaxation. I believe that the best way to reduce the effects of stress within your body is to learn how to daydream effectively. To begin with just find yourself a comfortable chair, disconnect the front-door bell, take the telephone off the hook and lie back with your eyes closed. Now while you are comfortable and peaceful allow your mind to drift back to some quiet and happy event in your past. It might be a favourite or much-enjoyed and well-remembered holiday. It may be a meeting or a picnic. It might be a day out on the beach. It doesn't matter what it is. Just sit or lie there with your eyes shut and the sound of the birds, the sea and the wind in your ears. Eventually you should be able to feel the sun on your face and the faint chattering of the people around you. Relaxing in this simple way will drastically cut the effects of stress on your body.

10. *Learn to think of the first signs of stomach trouble as early warning signs*.   If you suffer from heartburn, indigestion or wind then your body is simply passing on a message. You're pushing too hard and your stomach cannot stand the pace. Try and decide exactly what it is that is putting you under excessive pressure and try and decide how best to cope. You may need to cut back your exposure to stress or you may need to build up your own capacity to withstand stress.

Meanwhile you may find that the most effective way to deal with your stomach symptoms is to put into practice your mental and physical relaxation exercise. Minor stomach symptoms such as wind, indigestion, nausea and heartburn often get worse quite quickly and may continue for hours or even days if you make no attempt to protect yourself. Learn to watch for the first signs of any stomach trouble and to initiate immediately these aspects of your stress control programme.

The beauty of the counterstress programme is that you cannot lose. There are no side-effects — all you can do is benefit.

Index